ROSE | BIBLE B

The Bible
at a Glance

R&SE
PUBLISHING

Torrance, California

© 2008 Bristol Works, Inc.
Rose Publishing, Inc.
4733 Torrance Blvd., #259
Torrance, California 90503 U.S.A.
Email: info@rose-publishing.com
www.rose-publishing.com

Free, downloadable study guide at rose-publishing.com. Click on "News & Info," then on "Downloads."

Includes these Rose Publishing Titles:

Bible Overview © 2004, 2005 RW Research, Inc.
    Contributors: Shawn Vander Lugt, MDiv; Carol R. Witte
Bible Time Line © 2001, 2005 RW Research, Inc.
    Contributor: Timothy Paul Jones, EdD
How to Study the Bible © 2004, RW Research, Inc.
    Contributors: Shawn Vander Lugt, MDiv; Carol R. Witte
Then & Now Bible Maps © 2007 RW Research, Inc.
    Contributors: G. Goldsmith, Carol R. Witte
Where to Find Favorite Bible Verses © 2008 Bristol Works, Inc.
    Contributor: G. Goldsmith
Bible Promises © 2006 RW Research, Inc.
    Contributor: G. Goldsmith
Following Jesus © 2005 RW Research, Inc.
    Contributors: Sue Gilliland, G. Goldsmith, Carol R. Witte
Bible Translations Comparison © 2007 Bristol Works, Inc.
    Contributors: Vincent Botticelli; Gary Burge, PhD; G. Goldsmith;
    Timothy Paul Jones, EdD; Shawn Vander Lugt, MDiv
Many of these titles are available as individual pamphlets, as wall charts, and as ready-to-use PowerPoint® presentations.

Library of Congress Cataloging-in-Publication Data

The Bible at a glance.
    p. cm. – (Rose Bible basics)
  ISBN 978-1-59636-200-0 (pbk.)
  1. Bible–Criticism, interpretation, etc.–Miscellanea.
  BS511.3.B49 2008
  220.6'1–dc22
               2008007517

Printed in China

THE BIBLE AT A GLANCE

Contents

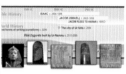

Continued on next page

→

THE BIBLE AT A GLANCE

Contents

Bible
Overview

OLD TESTAMENT	NEW TESTAMENT
The Law	Gospels & Acts
History	Paul's Letters (Epistles)
Poetry & Wisdom	
Major Prophets	General Epistles
Minor Prophets	Revelation

OLD TESTAMENT

THE LAW

The Law contains stories about the creation of the world, the flood, Abraham, Isaac, Jacob, the children of Israel in Egypt, the Exodus, and the time the children of Israel spent in the wilderness before entering the Promised Land. The books of the Law also recorded the law God gave to the people on Mt. Sinai which laid down the regulations for sacrifice, worship, and daily living. The Law is also called the Torah.

GENESIS

Who: Moses
What: The Beginnings
Where: Egypt and Canaan
When: c. 1450 BC–1400 BC
Why: To demonstrate that God is sovereign and loves his creation.

Outline (Chapter)
- Creation, Fall, and Flood (1-11)
- Abraham (11-25)
- Isaac and Jacob (25-36)
- Joseph (37-50)

Key Verse: I will establish my covenant as an everlasting covenant between me and you and your descendants after you for the generations to come, to be your God and the God of your descendants after you. (Genesis 17:7)

EXODUS

Who: Moses
What: Deliverance from Slavery
Where: Egypt and Canaan
When: c. 1445 BC–1440 BC
Why: To show God's faithfulness to the covenant and provide Israel with guidelines for healthy living.

Outline (Chapter)
- Moses (1-7)
- The Plagues (7-13)
- The Exodus (14-18)
- The Law (19-24)
- Tabernacle and Worship (25-40)

Key Verse: God said to Moses, "I am who I am. This is what you are to say to the Israelites: 'I AM has sent me to you'." (Exodus 3:14)

LEVITICUS

Who: Moses
What: Law and Sacrifice
Where: Sinai and Canaan
When: c. 1445 BC–1400 BC
Why: To instruct Israel on how to be holy and to be a blessing to others.

Outline (Chapter)
- Sacrifice (1-7)
- Priesthood (8-10)
- Clean and Unclean (11-15)
- Day of Atonement (16)
- Laws for Daily Life (17-27)

Key Verse: Consecrate yourselves and be holy, because I am the LORD your God. Keep my decrees and follow them. I am the LORD, who makes you holy. (Leviticus 20:7, 8)

NUMBERS

Who: Moses
What: Census and History
Where: Borders of Canaan
When: c. 1445 BC–1400 BC
Why: A reminder of what happens when people rebel against God

Outline (Chapter)
- Census (1-9)
- Sinai to Canaan (10-12)
- Spies and Rebellion (13-19)
- Moab (20-36)

Key Verse: The LORD bless you and keep you; the LORD make his face shine upon you and be gracious to you; the LORD turn his face toward you and give you peace. (Numbers 6:24-26)

DEUTERONOMY

Who: Moses
What: Servmons by Moses
Where: Plains of Moab
When: c. 1401 BC–1400 BC
Why: To remind the people what God expects from them.

Outline (Chapter)
- Sermon 1: Journey Review (1-4)
- Sermon 2: Laws (5-28)
- Sermon 3: Covenant (29-30)
- Final Farewells (31-34)

Key Verse: Hear, O Israel: The LORD our God, the LORD is one. Love the LORD your God with all your heart and with all your soul and with all your strength. (Deuteronomy 6:4, 5)

HISTORY

The 12 History books continue with the story of the people of Israel and the conquest of the Promised Land in the book of Joshua, the continuous cycle of disobedience in the book of Judges, the first kings and the United Kingdom, Divided Kingdom, the Assyrian invasion, Babylonian invasion, the years in exile, and the return from exile during the Persian rule.

JOSHUA

Who: Unknown (Joshua)
What: History of Conquest
Where: Canaan
When: c. 1405 BC–1383 BC
Why: To assure the people that obedience to God is rewarded.

Outline (Chapter)
• The Conquest (1-12)
• Dividing the Land (13-22)
• Joshua's Farewell (23-24)

Key Verse: Be strong and very courageous. Be careful to obey all the law my servant Moses gave you; do not turn from it to the right or to the left, that you may be successful wherever you go. (Joshua 1:7)

JUDGES

Who: Unknown (Samuel)
What: History before Kings
Where: Canaan
When: c. 1086 BC–1004 BC
Why: To stress the importance of remaining loyal to God.

Outline (Chapter)
• Reasons for Failure (1)
• The Judges: Othniel, Ehud, Shamgar, Deborah, Gideon, Tola, Jair, Jephthah, Ibzan, Elon, Abdon, and Samson (2-16)
• Days of Lawlessness (17-21)

Key Verse: In those days Israel had no king; everyone did as he saw fit. (Judges 21:25)

RUTH

Who: Unknown (Samuel)
What: Story of Faithful Foreigner
Where: Canaan
When: c. 1046 BC–1035 BC
Why: To demonstrate the kind of faithfulness, godliness, loyalty, and love that God desires for us.

Outline (Chapter)
• Naomi and Ruth (1)
• Ruth meets Boaz (2)
• The Threshing Floor (3)
• The Marriage (4)

Key Verse: But Ruth replied, "Don't urge me to leave you or to turn back from you. Where you go I will go, and where you stay I will stay. Your people will be my people and your God my God." (Ruth 1:16)

1 SAMUEL

Who: Unknown
What: History of Events
Where: Israel and Judah
When: c. 1050 BC–750 BC
Why: To record how Israel got a king.

Outline (Chapter)
• Samuel (1-7)
• Saul (8-15)
• Saul and David (16-31)

Key Verse: But Samuel replied: "Does the LORD delight in burnt offerings and sacrifices as much as in obeying the voice of the LORD? To obey is better than sacrifice, and to heed is better than the fat of rams." (1 Samuel 15:22)

2 SAMUEL

Who: Unknown
What: History of Events
Where: Israel and Judah
When: c. 1050 BC–750 BC
Why: To demonstrate the prominence of David's line.

Outline (Chapter)
• David's Reign in Judah (1-4)
• David Unites Israel (5-10)
• David and Bathsheba (11-12)
• Family Problems (13-20)
• Conclusions (21-24)

Key Verse: I have been with you wherever you have gone, and I have cut off all your enemies from before you. Now I will make your name great, like the names of the greatest men of the earth. (2 Samuel 7:9)

HISTORY

1 KINGS

Who: Unknown
What: Evaluation of the Kings
Where: In Exile in Babylon
When: 590 BC–570 BC
Why: To demonstrate the value of obeying and the danger of disobeying God.

Outline (Chapter)
- King Solomon's Reign (1-4)
- Temple Construction (5-8)
- Queen of Sheba (9-10)
- Kingdom Splits (11-16)
- Prophet Elijah (17-22)

Key Verse: So give your servant a discerning heart to govern your people and to distinguish between right and wrong. (1 Kings 3:9a)

2 KINGS

Who: Unknown
What: Evaluation of the Kings
Where: In Exile in Babylon
When: 590 BC–550 BC
Why: To demonstrate the value of obeying God.

Outline (Chapter)
- The Prophet Elisha (1-8)
- Kings of Judah and Israel (9-16)
- Fall of Israel (17-21)
- King Josiah (22-23)
- Fall of Judah; Exile (24-25)

Key Verse: And Hezekiah prayed to the LORD: "O LORD, God of Israel, enthroned between the cherubim, you alone are God over all the kingdoms of the earth. You have made heaven and earth." (2 Kings 19:15)

1 CHRONICLES

Who: Ezra
What: Review of David's Reign
Where: Judah
When: c. 450 BC–425 BC
Why: To encourage the remnant.

Key Verse: "Oh, that you would bless me and enlarge my territory! Let your hand be with me, and keep me from harm so that I will be free from pain." (1 Chronicles 4:10)

2 CHRONICLES

Who: Ezra
What: Highlights Kings of Judah
Where: Judah
When: c. 450 BC–425 BC
Why: To show the benefits that come from obedience.

Key Verse: As for us, the LORD is our God, and we have not forsaken him. (2 Chronicles 13:10a)

EZRA

Who: Ezra
What: History of Reconstruction
Where: Judah
When: c. 457 BC–444 BC
Why: Provide a detailed account of the exiles' return and the rebuilding of the Temple.

Outline (Chapter)
- The Exiles Return (1-2)
- Rebuilding the Temple (3-6)
- The Work of Ezra (7-10)

Key Verse: With praise and thanksgiving they sang to the Lord: "He is good; his love to Israel endures forever. And all the people gave a great shout of praise to the Lord, because the foundation of the house of the Lord was laid." (Ezra 3:11)

NEHEMIAH

Who: Nehemiah
What: History of Reconstruction
Where: Judah
When: c. 445 BC–430 BC
Why: Rebuilding of the walls of Jerusalem.

Outline (Chapter)
- Nehemiah Returns (1-2)
- The Rebuilding of the Walls (3)
- Threats and Persecution (4-7)
- Renewal of Covenant (8-10)
- Dedication and Laws (11-13)

Key Verse: Nehemiah said, "Go and enjoy choice food and sweet drinks, and send some to those who have nothing prepared. This day is sacred to our LORD. Do not grieve, for the joy of the LORD is your strength." (Nehemiah 8:10)

ESTHER

Who: Unknown
What: Story of Redemption
Where: Persia
When: c. 464 BC–435 BC
Why: To demonstrate that, in all circumstances, God is in control.

Outline (Chapter)
- Search for a new Queen (1-2)
- Haman's Plot (3)
- Esther's Plan (4-6)
- Haman's Downfall (7)
- Esther saves the Jews (8-10)

Key Verse: For if you remain silent at this time, relief and deliverance for the Jews will arise from another place, but you and your father's family will perish. And who knows but that you have come to royal position for such a time as this? (Esther 4:14)

POETRY & WISDOM

The five Poetry and Wisdom books include hymns, proverbs, poems, and dramas.

They illustrate the creative ways the people of Israel expressed themselves to God and to each other.

JOB

Who: Unknown
What: Story of Perseverance
Where: Mesopotamia (Uz)
When: Unknown
Why: To show the sovereignty of God and to illustrate faithfulness in the midst of suffering.

Outline (Chapter)
• Job Tested (1-3)
• Job's Friends (4-31)
• Elihu's Speech (32-37)
• God's Answer (38-42)

Key Verse: I know that my Redeemer lives, and that in the end he will stand upon the earth. And after my skin has been destroyed, yet in my flesh I will see God. (Job 19:25, 26)

PSALMS

Who: David, Moses, Asaph, Solomon, Ethan, Sons of Korah
What: Poetry and Song
Where: Ancient Israel
When: c. 1410 BC–430 BC
Why: To communicate with God and worship him.

Outline (Chapter)
• Book I: Psalms 1-41
• Book II: Psalms 42-72
• Book III: Psalms 73-89
• Book IV: Psalms 90-106
• Book V: Psalms 107-150

Key Verse: My mouth will speak in praise of the LORD. Let every creature praise his holy name for ever and ever. (Psalm 145:21)

PROVERBS

Who: Solomon and others
What: Wisdom
Where: Israel
When: c. 950 BC–700 BC
Why: To provide wisdom and guidance for God's children.

Outline (Chapter)
• Lessons in Wisdom (1-9)
• Proverbs of Solomon (10-22)
• Other Wise Sayings (23-24)
• Solomon's Sayings (25-29)
• Other Proverbs (30-31)

Key Verse: Trust in the LORD with all your heart and lean not on your own understanding; in all your ways acknowledge him, and he will make your paths straight. (Proverbs 3:5, 6)

ECCLESIASTES

Who: Solomon
What: Wisdom
Where: Jerusalem
When: c. 935 BC
Why: A search to discover truth.

Outline (Chapter)
• The Meaning of Life (1-2)
• Life is Not Always Fair (3-6)
• Wisdom (7-8)
• No One Knows the Future (9-10)
• Obedience to God (11-12)

Key Verse: Fear God and keep his commandments, for this is the whole duty of man. For God will bring every deed into judgment, including every hidden thing, whether it is good or evil. (Ecclesiastes 12:13, 14)

SONG OF SOLOMON

Who: Solomon
What: Love Poem
Where: Jerusalem
When: c. 965 BC
Why: To illustrate the joy of authentic love found in marriage.

Outline (Chapter)
• The Courtship (1-3)
• The Wedding (3-4)
• The Lasting Relationship (5-8)

Key Verse: Many waters cannot quench love; rivers cannot wash it away. If one were to give all the wealth of his house for love, it would be utterly scorned. (Song of Solomon 8:7)

MAJOR PROPHETS

The five Major Prophets are not called "major" because of their message or quality, but rather because of the length of the books. The prophets brought God's word which included warning of judgment, warnings and hope for the immediate future (as well as warnings and hope for the distant future), and hope in the coming Messiah.

ISAIAH

Who: Isaiah
What: Prophecy and Judgement
Where: Judah
When: c. 740 BC–680 BC
Why: To convince the people that salvation was possible through repentance and hope in the coming Messiah.

Outline (Chapter)
• Condemnation (1-39)
• Comfort in Exile (40-55)
• Future Hope (56-66)

Key Verse: For to us a child is born, to us a son is given, and the government will be on his shoulders. And he will be called Wonderful Counselor, Mighty God, Everlasting Father, Prince of Peace. (Isaiah 9:6)

JEREMIAH

Who: Jeremiah
What: Prophecy and Judgement
Where: Judah
When: c. 626 BC–580 BC
Why: To warn Judah of their destruction, to remind them of their sin, and convince them to submit to the Babylonian invaders.

Outline (Chapter)
• Jeremiah (1-10)
• Prophetic Warnings (11-28)
• New Covenant (29-39)
• The Fall of Jerusalem (40-52)

Key Verse: "For I know the plans I have for you," declares the LORD, "plans to prosper you and not to harm you, plans to give you hope and a future." (Jeremiah 29:11)

LAMENTATIONS

Who: Jeremiah
What: Dirge Poem (Lament)
Where: Babylon
When: c. 586 BC–584 BC
Why: To express the despair of the people of Judah over the loss of their land, city, and Temple.

Outline (Chapter)
• Sorrows of Captives (1)
• Anger with Jerusalem (2)
• Hope and Mercy (3)
• Punishment (4)
• Restoration (5)

Key Verse: Because of the LORD's great love we are not consumed, for his compassions never fail. They are new every morning; great is your faithfulness. (Lamentations 3:22, 23)

EZEKIEL

Who: Ezekiel
What: Prophecy and Warning
Where: Babylon
When: c. 587 BC–565 BC
Why: To confront people about their sin, give them one last chance to repent, and offer hope.

Outline (Chapter)
• Ezekiel (1-3)
• Judgment of Judah (4-24)
• Judgment on the Nations (25-32)
• The End of the Age (33-39)
• Restoration of Temple (40-48)

Key Verse: I will give you a new heart and put a new spirit in you; I will remove from you your heart of stone and give you a heart of flesh. (Ezekiel 36:26)

DANIEL

Who: Daniel
What: Prophecy and Apocalyptic
Where: Babylon
When: c. 605 BC–530 BC
Why: To convince the Jewish exiles that God is sovereign and to provide them with a vision of their future redemption.

Outline (Chapter)
• Daniel and His Friends (1-6)
• Apocalyptic Visions (7-12)

Key Verse: In the time of those kings, the God of heaven will set up a kingdom that will never be destroyed, nor will it be left to another people. It will crush all those kingdoms and bring them to an end, but it will itself endure forever. (Daniel 2:44)

MINOR PROPHETS

The 12 Minor Prophets, called "The Book of the Twelve" in the Hebrew Bible, are just as important as the Major Prophets. They are called "minor" because of the shorter length of the books. The Minor Prophets also brought God's word to the people regarding judgment and hope.

HOSEA

Who: Hosea
What: Prophecy and Warning
Where: Israel
When: c. 755 BC–710 BC
Why: To illustrate Israel's spiritual adultery and warn of destruction.

Outline (Chapter)
• The Unfaithful Wife (1-3)
• The Unfaithful Nation (4-14)

Key Verse: Because you have rejected knowledge, I also reject you as my priests; because you have ignored the law of your God, I also will ignore your children. (Hosea 4:6)

JOEL

Who: Joel
What: Prophecy and Judgment
Where: Judah
When: Unknown
Why: To call Judah to repentance in order to avoid judgment.

Outline (Chapter)
• Locusts (1)
• Blessings and Curses (2-3)

Key Verse: And afterward, I will pour out my Spirit on all people. Your sons and daughters will prophesy, your old men will dream dreams, your young men will see visions. (Joel 2:28b)

AMOS

Who: Amos
What: Prophecy and Judgment
Where: Israel
When: c. 760 BC–750 BC
Why: To accuse and judge Israel for injustice and lack of mercy.

Outline (Chapter)
• Neighbors Punished (1-3)
• Israel's Destruction (3-8)
• Future Hope (9)

Key Verse: Seek good, not evil, that you may live. Then the Lord God Almighty will be with you, just as you say he is. (Amos 5:14)

OBADIAH

Who: Obadiah
What: Prophecy
Where: Judah
When: c. 586 BC
Why: To prophesy against Edom.

Outline: (Verses)
• Judgment on Edom (1-9)
• Edom's Violations (10-14)
• Israel's Victory (15-21)

Key Verse: Because of the violence against your brother Jacob, you will be covered with shame; you will be destroyed forever. (Obadiah 10)

JONAH

Who: Jonah
What: Story of God's Mercy
Where: Nineveh
When: c. 783 BC–753 BC
Why: To show that God loves all.

Outline (Chapter)
• Jonah Flees (1)
• Jonah Prays (2)
• Jonah's Anger with God's Mercy

Key Verse: I knew that you are a gracious and compassionate God, slow to anger and abounding in love, a God who relents from sending calamity. (Jonah 4:2b)

MICAH

Who: Micah
What: Prophecy and Judgment
Where: Israel and Judah
When: c. 739 BC–686 BC
Why: To warn people of judgment and to offer hope.

Outline (Chapter)
• Judgment and Deliverance (1-5)
• Confession and Restoration (6-7)

Key Verse: He has showed you, O man, what is good. And what does the Lord require of you? To act justly and to love mercy and to walk humbly with your God. (Micah 6:8)

MINOR PROPHETS

NAHUM

Who: Nahum
What: Prophecy and Judgment
Where: Judah and Nineveh
When: c. 664 BC–612 BC
Why: To pronounce judgment on Nineveh and the Assyrian Empire.

Outline (Chapter)
• Judgment (1)
• Hope for Judah (1)
• Nineveh's Destruction (2-3)

Key Verse: The LORD is good, a refuge in times of trouble. He cares for those who trust in him. (Nahum 1:7)

HABAKKUK

Who: Habakkuk
What: Prophecy and Judgment
Where: Judah
When: c. 609 BC–597 BC
Why: To affirm that the wicked will not prevail and to remind Judah that God is in control.

Outline (Chapter)
• Tough Questions (1-2)
• Praise to the Lord (3)

Key Verse: ...yet I will rejoice in the LORD, I will be joyful in God my Savior. (Habakkuk 3:18)

ZEPHANIAH

Who: Zephaniah
What: Prophecy and Judgment
Where: Judah
When: c. 640 BC–628 BC
Why: To motivate repentance.

Outline (Chapter)
• Judgment on Judah (1)
• Judgment on the Nations (2)
• Promise of Restoration (3)

Key Verse: The great day of the LORD is near—near and coming quickly. Listen! The cry on the day of the LORD will be bitter, the shouting of the warrior there. (Zephaniah 1:14)

HAGGAI

Who: Haggai
What: Prophecy and Hope
Where: Judah
When: c. 520 BC
Why: To urge the people to complete rebuilding the Temple.

Outline (Chapter)
• Rebuild Temple (1)
• Blessings (2)
• David's Throne (2)

Key Verse: This is what I covenanted with you when you came out of Egypt. And my Spirit remains among you. Do not fear. (Haggai 2:5)

ZECHARIAH

Who: Zechariah
What: Prophecy and Hope
Where: Judah
When: c. 520 BC–519 BC
Why: To give hope to the remnant.

Outline (Chapter)
• Zechariah's Visions (1-8)
• Messianic Prophecy (9-12)

Key Verse: Rejoice greatly, O Daughter of Zion! Shout, Daughter of Jerusalem! See, your king comes to you, righteous and having salvation, gentle and riding on a donkey, on a colt, the foal of a donkey. (Zechariah 9:9)

MALACHI

Who: Malachi
What: Prophecy and Judgment
Where: Judah
When: c. 430 BC–400 BC
Why: To examine Judah's actions and make sure God has priority.

Outline (Chapter)
• Sins Identified (1-3)
• Rewards for the Righteous (4)

Key Verse: But for you who revere my name, the sun of righteousness will rise with healing in its wings. (Malachi 4:2)

NEW TESTAMENT GOSPELS & ACTS

The Gospels, which are the first four books of the New Testament, record the good news of God's plan for a Savior through the life, ministry, death, and resurrection of Jesus Christ. Each writer has a particular method or style to communicate the life and message of Jesus Christ.

Acts is the record of the radically changed "acts" or "actions" of the followers of Jesus Christ after the resurrection. Acts opens with the out-flowing of the Holy Spirit and describes the missionary efforts of the early followers of Jesus as they spread the message of the gospel to Judea and Samaria. Acts also records the actions of the apostle Paul as he and other courageous believers continued to spread the good news of Jesus to the Jews and Gentiles of the Roman Empire.

MATTHEW

Who: Matthew (also called Levi)
What: Gospel
Where: Judea
When: c. AD 60
Why: To show Jesus as the Son of David, the Kingly Messiah who fulfills prophecy.
Outline (Chapter)
• Birth and Early Life (1-4)
• Ministry of Christ (5-20)
• Death and Resurrection (21-28)
Key Verse: Then Jesus came to them and said, "All authority in heaven and on earth has been given to me. Therefore go and make disciples of all nations, baptizing them in the name of the Father and of the Son and of the Holy Spirit." (Matthew 28:18-19)

MARK

Who: John Mark
What: Gospel
Where: Rome
When: c. AD 58
Why: To show Jesus as the Suffering Son of Man sent to serve and not be served.
Outline (Chapter)
• Introduction (1)
• Ministry of Christ (2-10)
• Death and Resurrection (11-16)
Key Verse: ...Instead, whoever wants to become great among you must be your servant, and whoever wants to be first must be slave of all. For even the Son of Man did not come to be served, but to serve, and to give his life as a ransom for many. (Mark 10:43-45)

LUKE

Who: Luke (The Physician)
What: Gospel
Where: Caesarea
When: c. AD 60–AD 62
Why: To show Jesus as the Savior of the World who has compassion for all human beings.
Outline (Chapter)
• Birth and Early Life (1-4)
• Ministry of Christ (5-19)
• Death and Resurrection (20-24)
Key Verse: Then he said to them all: "If anyone would come after me, he must deny himself and take up his cross daily and follow me. For whoever wants to save his life will lose it, but whoever loses his life for me will save it." (Luke 9:23,24)

JOHN

Who: John (The Beloved Disciple)
What: Gospel
Where: Asia Minor
When: c. AD 85–AD 95
Why: To show Jesus as the Son of God, the Word made flesh, who provides eternal life for all who believe in him.
Outline (Chapter)
• Introduction (1)
• Ministry of Christ (2-12)
• Private Ministry (13-17)
• Death and Resurrection (18-21)
Key Verse: For God so loved the world that he gave his one and only Son, that whoever believes in him shall not perish but have eternal life. (John 3:16)

ACTS

Who: Luke (The Physician)
What: History of Early Church
Where: Caesarea and Rome
When: c. AD 60–AD 62
Why: To record how the Holy Spirit acted through believers to spread the Word of God.
Outline (Chapter)
• Jerusalem (1-8)
• Judea and Samaria (8-12)
• Paul's Journeys (13-20)
• Paul Taken to Rome (21-28)
Key Verse: But you will receive power when the Holy Spirit comes on you; and you will be my witnesses in Jerusalem, and in all Judea and Samaria, and to the ends of the earth. (Acts 1:8)

PAUL'S LETTERS (EPISTLES)

The apostle Paul wrote 13 letters to young churches, pastors, and friends in order to guide, encourage, and correct them. Most of these letters served a specific purpose or addressed a specific question or problem.

ROMANS

Who: Paul
What: Letter to Roman Christians
Where: Corinth
When: C. AD 57
Why: To illustrate law, faith, and salvation, and righteous living.
Outline (Chapter)
- Christian Gospel (1-8)
- Israel (9-11)
- Christian Life (12-16)

Key Verse: Therefore, I urge you, brothers, in view of God's mercy, to offer your bodies as living sacrifices, holy and pleasing to God—this is your spiritual act of worship. Do not conform any longer to the pattern of this world, but be transformed by the renewing of your mind. (Romans 12:1, 2a)

1 CORINTHIANS

Who: Paul
What: Letter to Church in Corinth
Where: Ephesus
When: C. AD 56
Why: To address division and immorality and to encourage them to love each other.
Outline (Chapter)
- Divisions (1-4)
- Morality (5-11)
- Spiritual Gifts (12-14)
- The Resurrection (15-16)

Key Verse: Love is patient, love is kind. It does not envy, it does not boast, it is not proud. It is not rude, it is not self-seeking, it is not easily angered, it keeps no record of wrongs. (1 Corinthians 13:4, 5)

2 CORINTHIANS

Who: Paul
What: Letter to Church in Corinth
Where: Philippi
When: C. AD 56
Why: To defend Paul's call as an apostle, to address deceivers.
Outline (Chapter)
- Apostolic Characteristics (1-7)
- Giving (8-9)
- Paul's Defense (10-13)

Key Verse: But he said to me, "My grace is sufficient for you, for my power is made perfect in weakness." Therefore I will boast all the more gladly about my weaknesses, so that Christ's power may rest on me. (2 Corinthians 12:9)

GALATIANS

Who: Paul
What: Letter to Churches in Galatia
Where: Asia Minor
When: C. AD 50–AD 55
Why: To warn against legalism and defend justification by faith as well as Paul's apostolic authority.
Outline (Chapter)
- Paul's Defense (1-2)
- Justification by Faith (3-4)
- The Christian Life (5-6)

Key Verse: But the fruit of the Spirit is love, joy, peace, patience, kindness, goodness, faithfulness, gentleness and self-control. Against such things there is no law. (Galatians 5:22, 23)

EPHESIANS

Who: Paul
What: Letter to Church in Ephesus
Where: Prison in Rome
When: C. AD 60–AD 64
Why: To show believers what it means to be a follower of Christ and encourage them in their spiritual walk.
Outline (Chapter)
- Spiritual Blessings (1-3)
- The Christian Life (4-6)

Key Verse: For it is by grace you have been saved, through faith—and this not from yourselves, it is the gift of God—not by works, so that no one can boast. (Ephesians 2:8, 9)

PHILIPPIANS

Who: Paul
What: Letter to Church in Philippi
Where: Prison in Rome
When: C. AD 60–AD 64
Why: To express Paul's love and affection for the Philippians.

Outline (Chapter)
- Joy of Life (1)
- Humility of Christ (2)
- Finish the Race (3)
- Thanks and Greetings (4)

Key Verse: Do everything without complaining or arguing, so that you may become blameless and pure, children of God without fault in a crooked and depraved generation, in which you shine like stars in the universe. (Philippians 2:14, 15)

COLOSSIANS

Who: Paul
What: Letter to Church in Colossae
Where: Prison in Rome
When: C. AD 60–AD 64
Why: To counteract heretical teachings and exhort believers

Outline (Chapter)
- Thanksgiving (1)
- Work of Christ (1-2)
- Finish the Race (3-4)
- Final Greetings (4)

Key Verse: For in Christ all the fullness of the Deity lives in bodily form, and you have been given fullness in Christ, who is the head over every power and authority. (Colossians 2:9, 10)

PAUL'S LETTERS (EPISTLES)

1 THESSALONIANS

Who: Paul

What: Letter to the Church in Thessalonica

Where: Corinth

When: c. AD 49–AD 54

Why: To emphasize Christ's return and to stress commitment.

Outline (Chapter)
- Faith and Example (1-3)
- Living for God (4)
- Christ's Return (4-5)

Key Verse: Be joyful always; pray continually; give thanks in all circumstances, for this is God's will for you in Christ Jesus. Do not put out the Spirit's fire; do not treat prophecies with contempt. Test everything. Hold on to the good. Avoid every kind of evil. May God himself, the God of peace, sanctify you through and through. May your whole spirit, soul and body be kept blameless at the coming of our Lord Jesus Christ. (1 Thess. 5:16-23)

2 THESSALONIANS

Who: Paul

What: Letter to the Church in Thessalonica

Where: Corinth

When: c. AD 50–AD 54

Why: To emphasize Christ's return and to encourage believers.

Outline (Chapter)
- Praise and Encouragement (1)
- Christ's Return (2)
- Pray and Work (3)

Key Verse: We have confidence in the Lord that you are doing and will continue to do the things we command. May the Lord direct your hearts into God's love and Christ's perseverance. In the name of the Lord Jesus Christ, we command you, brothers, to keep away from every brother who is idle and does not live according to the teaching you received from us. (2 Thessalonians 3:4-6)

1 TIMOTHY

Who: Paul

What: Letter to Timothy

Where: Rome

When: c. AD 64

Why: To remove false doctrine and suggest proper leadership for the church in Ephesus.

Outline (Chapter)
- Trouble in Ephesus (1)
- Church Leadership (2-3)
- False Teachers (4)
- Discipline (5)
- Paul's Advice to Timothy (6)

Key Verse: Don't let anyone look down on you because you are young, but set an example for the believers in speech, in life, in love, in faith and in purity. Until I come, devote yourself to the public reading of Scripture, to preaching and to teaching. (1 Timothy 4:12, 13)

2 TIMOTHY

Who: Paul

What: Letter to Timothy

Where: Prison in Rome

When: c. AD 65–AD 67

Why: To encourage Timothy to remain faithful in ministry even in the midst of suffering.

Outline (Chapter)
- Thanksgiving (1)
- Call to Remain Faithful (2)
- Authority of God's Word (3)
- Lead a Godly Life (3-4)

Key Verse: ...from infancy you have known the holy Scriptures, which are able to make you wise for salvation through faith in Christ Jesus. All Scripture is God-breathed and is useful for teaching, rebuking, correcting and training in righteousness, so that the man of God may be thoroughly equipped for every good work. (2 Tim. 3:15-17)

TITUS

Who: Paul

What: Letter to Titus

Where: Rome

When: c. AD 64

Why: To encourage the church in Crete to do good works.

Outline (Chapter)
- Instruction for Titus (1)
- Living the Faith (2-3)
- Final Instructions (3)

Key Verse: But when the kindness and love of God our Savior appeared, he saved us, not because of righteous things we had done, but because of his mercy. He saved us through the washing of rebirth and renewal by the Holy Spirit, whom he poured out on us generously through Jesus Christ our Savior, so that, having been justified by his grace, we might become heirs having the hope of eternal life. (Titus 3:4-7)

PHILEMON

Who: Paul

What: Letter to Philemon

Where: Prison in Rome

When: c. AD 60

Why: To appeal to Philemon to forgive and receive Onesimus, a runaway slave.

Outline (Verses)
- Salutations (1-3)
- Philemon's Love and Faith (4-7)
- Paul's Appeal (8-22)
- Final Greetings (22-25)

Key Verse: So if you consider me a partner, welcome him as you would welcome me. If he has done you any wrong or owes you anything, charge it to me. I, Paul, am writing this with my own hand. I will pay it back–not to mention that you owe me your very self. (Philemon 17-19)

GENERAL EPISTLES & REVELATION

The eight General Epistles were written by other apostles and leaders including Simon Peter, James, John, and Jude. The General Epistles were addressed to the early Christians to provide guidance, encouragement through persecution, and warnings of false teachings.

HEBREWS

Who: Unknown (Paul)
What: Letter to Hebrew Believers
Where: Unknown
When: c. AD 60–AD 69
Why: To emphasize the superiority of Christ over the Old Covenant.

Outline (Chapter)
• Supremacy of Christ (1-4)
• The New Covenant (4-10)
• The Life of Faith (11-13)

Key Verse: Let us fix our eyes on Jesus, the author and perfecter of our faith, who for the joy set before him endured the cross, scorning its shame, and sat down at the right hand of the throne of God. (Hebrews 12:2)

JAMES

Who: James
What: Letter to Jewish Believers
Where: Jerusalem
When: c. AD 48
Why: Encouragement to live out one's faith within the Christian community.

Outline (Chapter)
• Living a Life of Faith (1-2)
• Faith without Works (2-3)
• Speech and Wisdom (3-4)

Key Verse: My dear brothers, take note of this: Everyone should be quick to listen, slow to speak and slow to become angry, for man's anger does not bring about the righteous life that God desires. (James 1:19, 20)

1 PETER

Who: Peter
What: Letter to All Christians
Where: Rome
When: c. AD 64–AD 65
Why: To call Christians to holiness.
Outline (Chapter)
• Holiness and Submission (1-2)
• Suffering (3-4)
Key Verse: The end of all things is near. Therefore be clear minded and self-controlled so that you can pray. (1 Peter 4:7)

2 PETER

Who: Peter
What: Letter to All Christians
Where: Rome
When: c. AD 64–AD 70
Why: To warn against false teachers.
Outline (Chapter)
• Living Like Christ; False Teachers (1-2)
• The Return of Christ (3)
Key Verse: For prophecy never had its origin in the will of man, but men spoke from God as they were carried along by the Holy Spirit. (2 Peter 1:21)

1 JOHN

Who: John
What: Letter to All Christians
Where: Ephesus
When: c. AD 85–AD 95
Why: To emphasize love in Christ.
Outline (Chapter)
• Living in the Light (1-2)
• Living in Love (3-4)
• Living by Faith (5)
Key Verse: Whoever does not love does not know God, because God is love. (1 John 4:8)

2 JOHN

Who: John
What: Letter to the Elect Lady
Where: Ephesus
When: c. AD 85–AD 95
Why: To warn against heresy and false teachers

Key Verse: Watch out that you do not lose what you have worked for, but that you may be rewarded fully. (2 John 8)

3 JOHN

Who: John
What: Letter to Gaius
Where: Ephesus
When: c. AD 85–AD 95
Why: To praise Gaius for his loyalty to the truth and criticize Diotrephes for his pride.

Key Verse: I have no greater joy than to hear that my children are walking in the truth. (3 John 4)

JUDE

Who: Jude
What: Letter to all Christians
Where: Unknown
When: c. AD 60–AD 95
Why: To warn against heresy

Key Verse: To him who is able to keep you from falling and to present you before his glorious presence without fault and with great joy. (Jude 24)

The book of Revelation addressed seven churches in Asia Minor (Turkey today). It encourages believers who are experiencing persecution. Revelation illustrates that God is in control and that all people were created to love and worship God.

REVELATION

Who: John
What: Letter to Seven Churches
Where: Island of Patmos
When: c. AD 96 or c. AD 69
Why: To give hope to persecuted Christians and provide a vision of Christ's return.

Outline (Chapter)
• The Seven Churches (1-4)
• Visions (5-16)
• God's Triumph (17-20)
• The New Creation (21-22)

Key Verse: Then I saw a new heaven and a new earth, for the first heaven and the first earth had passed away, and there was no longer any sea. (Revelation 21:1)

Bible
Time Line

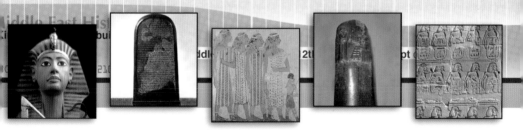

BC	2100 BC	2000 BC	1900 BC

Bible History

ISAAC c. 2066-1886

JACOB (ISRAEL) c. 2005-1859

JACOB FLEES TO HARAN c. 1929 ○

World History

est forms of writing (cuneiform) c. 3200   ○ The city of Ur falls c. 2004

First Ziggurats built by Ur-Nammu c. 2112-2095

Middle East History

300 Key People & Events in the Bible

Genesis to Revelation

2200 BC — AD 100

Compare Bible, World & Middle East History

Creation to Abraham

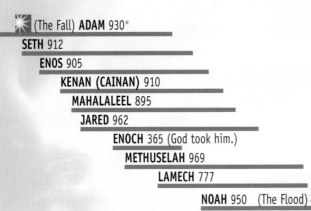

(The Fall) **ADAM** 930*
SETH 912
ENOS 905
KENAN (CAINAN) 910
MAHALALEEL 895
JARED 962
ENOCH 365 (God took him.)
METHUSELAH 969
LAMECH 777
NOAH 950   (The Flood)
SHEM 600
ARPHAXAD 438
SALAH 433
EBER 464
PELEG 239
REU 239
SERUG 230
NAHOR 148
TERAH 205
ABRAHAM 175

* The numbers indicate the age of the person at death.
The red lines indicate the life span of the person in
relationship to the others.

Key

Major event

C. Circa (about)

  10 years between vertical lines

o Year marker

Time span marker

Many dates listed are approximate and may vary according to different scholars.

Books of the Bible are listed by date of events on the TIME LINE. →   GENESIS, JOB

2200 BC	2100 BC

Abraham to the Sojourn in Egypt

Bible History

ABRAHAM c. 2166-1991
Some scholars place Abraham's birth at 1952 BC.
In this case, biblical events through Joseph would
slide to the right 214 years.

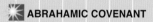 **ABRAHAMIC COVENANT**

ISHMAEL c. 2080-1943

ISAAC c. 2066-1886

JACOB (ISRAEL) c. 2005-1859

World History

The city of Ur falls c. 2004 ○

First Ziggurats built by Ur-Nammu c. 2112-2095

Earliest forms of writing (cuneiform) c. 3200

EGYPT

Old Kingdom Pyramids built c. 2700-2200

**Middle Kingdom
(11th-12th Dynasty)
in Egypt** c. 2050-1800

Middle East History

2200 BC	2100 BC

THE BRONZE AGE

GENESIS, JOB

2000 BC	1900 BC

Abraham to the Sojourn in Egypt

JOSEPH c. 1914-1805

O **JOSEPH
BECOMES AN OFFICIAL IN EGYPT**
c. 1884

O **JACOB AND HIS FAMILY GO TO EGYPT**
c. 1876
Sons of Jacob (Israel)-Reuben, Simeon, Levi,
Judah, Dan, Naphtali, Gad, Asher, Issachar,
Zebulun, Joseph, Benjamin
Grandsons (sons of Joseph)-Manasseh,
Ephraim

O **JOB** (dates unknown)

ISHMAEL   c. 2080-1943

ISAAC c. 2066-1886

JACOB (ISRAEL) c. 2005-1859

O **JACOB FLEES TO HARAN** c. 1929

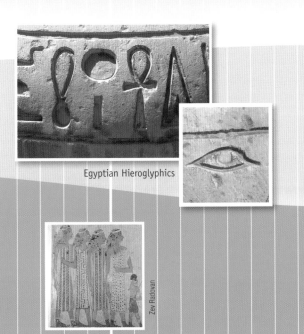

Egyptian Hieroglyphics

Zev Radovan

Beni Hasan Mural

Middle Kingdom (11th-12th Dynasty) in Egypt c. 2050-1800

2000 BC	1900 BC

THE BRONZE AGE

GENESIS, JOB

1800 BC   1700 BC

Abraham to the Sojourn in Egypt

The Gilgamesh Epic

Zev Radovan, Jerusalem

Zev Radovan, Jerusalem

Hammurapi (Hammurabi) reigns in Babylon 1792-1750

○ **Law code of Hammurapi** ·

Code of Hammurapi

Egyptian Monuments

L. Jeans-Shaw

Hyksos rule Egypt c. 1670-1570

Second Intermediate Period (13th-17th Dynasties) begins c. 1800-1570

1800 BC   1700 BC

THE BRONZE AGE

GENESIS, JOB

EXODUS,
LEVITICUS, NUMBERS,
DEUTERONOMY, JOSHUA

1600 BC   1500 BC

Moses and the Exodus

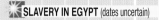SLAVERY IN EGYPT (dates uncertain)

AARON c. 1529-1407

MOSES c. 1526-1406

FIRST PASSOVER c. 1446

"HIGH DATE" FOR THE EXODUS & WILDERNESS WANDERINGS c. 1446

TEN COMMANDMENTS AND OTHER LAWS GIVEN

Tabernacle

TABERNACLE

JOSHUA LEADS ISRAELITES INTO CANAAN

RAHAB HELPS SAVE SPIES ○

Stan Stein

○**Hittites sack Babylon** 1595

Shang Dynasty in China c. 1450-1027

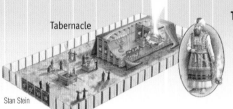

Ruins at Jericho

○**18th Dynasty begins in Egypt** 1570

Ahmose 1570-1545

Amenhotep 1545-1529

Thutmose 1529-1517

Thutmose II 1517-1504

Thutmose III 1504-1453

Queen Hatshepshut 1504-1483

Hyksos rule Egypt c. 1670-1570

Amenhotep II 1453-1426

Thutmose IV 1426-1416

Second Intermediate Period (13th-17th Dynasties) begins c. 1800-1570

1600 BC   1500 BC

THE IRON AGE

| EXODUS, LEVITICUS, NUMBERS, DEUTERONOMY, JOSHUA | JUDGES, RUTH, 1 & 2 SAMUEL, 1 CHRONICLES, PSALMS |

1400 BC   1300 BC

The Conquest and the Judges

 ERA OF THE JUDGES BEGINS c. 1350
Judges: Othniel, Ehud, Shamgar, Deborah (and Barak), Gideon, Tola, Jair, Jephthah, Ibzan, Elon, Abdon, Samson, Eli, and Samuel

○**RUTH**

"LOW DATE" FOR THE EXODUS c. 1290
Some scholars date the Exodus at 1290. For a "low date" Exodus, the dates of the Passover, wilderness wandering events, and the beginning date for the era of the Judges would slide to the right 156 years, compressing the dates of the Judges.

Shang Dynasty in China c. 1450-1027

King Tutankhamen

Zev Radovan

Merneptah Stele

Amenhotep III 1416-1377

Amenhotep IV (Ikhnaton) 1377-1360

Tutankhamen ("King Tut") 1360-1350

Ay 1350-1347

Horemhab 1347-1318

○**19th Dynasty begins in Egypt** 1318

Rameses I 1318-1317

Seti I 1317-1304

Merneptah
1237-1227

Pharaoh Merneptah's victory stele mentions Israel for the first time in non-biblical history

Rameses II 1304-1237

1400 BC   1300 BC

THE IRON AGE

JUDGES, RUTH, 1 & 2 SAMUEL, 1 CHRONICLES, PSALMS

1200 BC	1100 BC

The Conquest and the Judges   United Kingdom

PRIESTHOOD OF ABIATHAR

ERA OF THE JUDGES

KINGS OF ISRAEL
(listed by dates of reign)

ELI, PRIEST IN SHILOH
c. 1100-1060

KING SAUL c. 1051-1011

KING DAVID
c. 1011-971

SAMUEL, JUDGE & PROPHET OF ISRAEL c. 1060-1020

○ **Iron Age begins; Hittite Empire collapses** c.1200

Shang Dynasty in China c. 1450-1027

○ **Trojan War Begins** c.1190

Tiglath-Pileser I rules Assyria 1114-1076

○ **Chou Dynasty begins in China** c. 1150-256

○

Mayan Dynasties founded in Central America c.1000

○ **Egypt's power begins to decline** c. 1164

1200 BC	1100 BC

THE IRON AGE

1 KINGS, ECCLESIASTES, SONG OF SOLOMON, PROVERBS, 2 CHRONICLES, 2 KINGS

1000 BC   900 BC

United Kingdom   Divided Kingdom

ABIATHAR
NATHAN

JEROBOAM I 931-910   **AHAB** 874-853
          NADAB 910-909
                    AHAZIAH 853-852
          BAASHA 909-886
                    ELAH 886-885   **JORAM (JEHORAM)** 852-841
                    ○ **ZIMRI** 885
                                                JEHU 841-814
                    TIBNI 885-880
                    OMRI 885-874   **JEHOAHAZ** 814-798

KING DAVID

KINGS OF ISRAEL (NORTHERN)

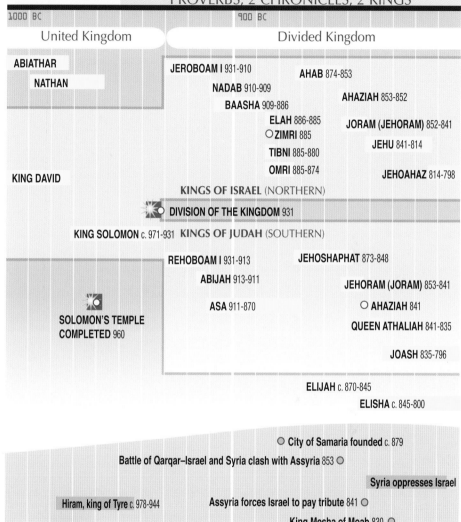

○ **DIVISION OF THE KINGDOM** 931

KING SOLOMON c. 971-931 **KINGS OF JUDAH** (SOUTHERN)

REHOBOAM I 931-913   **JEHOSHAPHAT** 873-848
          ABIJAH 913-911
                    JEHORAM (JORAM) 853-841
          ASA 911-870   ○ **AHAZIAH** 841
                    QUEEN ATHALIAH 841-835

**SOLOMON'S TEMPLE
COMPLETED** 960
                    JOASH 835-796

ELIJAH c. 870-845
          ELISHA c. 845-800

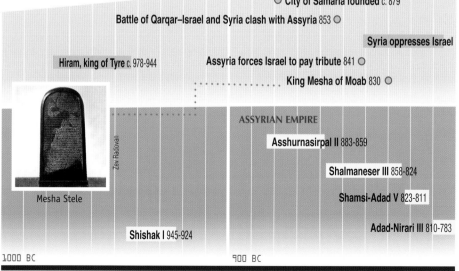

○ City of Samaria founded c. 879

Battle of Qarqar–Israel and Syria clash with Assyria 853 ○

Syria oppresses Israel

Hiram, king of Tyre c. 978-944   Assyria forces Israel to pay tribute 841 ○

King Mesha of Moab 830 ○

ASSYRIAN EMPIRE

Asshurnasirpal II 883-859

Shalmaneser III 858-824

Shamsi-Adad V 823-811

Mesha Stele

Zev Radovan

Adad-Nirari III 810-783

Shishak I 945-924

1000 BC   900 BC

THE IRON AGE

JONAH, AMOS, ISAIAH,
HOSEA, MICAH

NAHUM, JEREMIAH, LAMENTATIONS,
ZEPHANIAH, DANIEL, EZEKIEL,...

800 BC   700 BC

Divided Kingdom

JEHOASH 798-782
    JEROBOAM II 793-753
        ○ZECHARIAH 753
        ○SHALLUM 752
        MENAHEM 752-742
           PEKAHIAH 742-740
       PEKAH 752-732
KINGS OF ISRAEL (NORTHERN) HOSHEA 732-722

○ISRAEL (NORTHERN KINGDOM) FALLS TO THE ASSYRIANS 722
      NAHUM c. 658-615
        JEREMIAH c. 650-582
      ZEPHANIAH c. 640-626
        HABAKKUK c. 608-598
         EZEKIEL
         DANIEL

KINGS OF JUDAH (SOUTHERN)
AMAZIAH 796-767
  UZZIAH (AZARIAH) 792-740
      JOTHAM 750-732
        AHAZ (JEHOAHAZ) 735-716
          HEZEKIAH 716-687
         MANASSEH 697-643
JOASH 835-796

      JEHOAHAZ (SHALLUM) 609 ○
      JEHOIAKIM (ELIAKIM) 609-598
    FIRST EXILE OF JEWS TO BABYLON 605 ○
        AMON 643-641
        JOSIAH 641-609

○JONAH c. 781
  AMOS c. 765-754
      Nineveh, capital of Assyria, falls to the Babylonians and the Medes 612 ○
    ISAIAH c. 760-673
    HOSEA c. 758-725
      MICAH c. 738-698

○ First recorded Olympic games 776
  ○ Traditional date for the founding of Rome 753
Homer c. 800-701   Assyria rules Egypt 671-652

...ASSYRIAN EMPIRE
      Shalmaneser V 726-722
  Shalmaneser IV 783-773
      Sargon II (722-705) takes Samaria, exiles people to Babylon 722
    Ashurdan III 772-755
      Sennacherib 704-681
    Ashur-Nirari V 754-745
      Esarhaddon 680-669
Adad-Nirari III 810-783
    Tiglath-Pileser III 744-727
      Asshurbanipal 668-627
        Nabopolassar I 625-605

THE IRON AGE

... HABAKKUK, OBADIAH,
ZECHARIAH, HAGGAI

ESTHER, MALACHI, EZRA,
JOEL, NEHEMIAH

600 BC

500 BC

Exile

Restoration of Jerusalem

ZECHARIAH c. 522-509
HAGGAI c. 520

OBADIAH c. 590

**CYRUS'S EDICT ALLOWS JEWS TO RETURN
TO THEIR LAND** 538
EXILES BEGIN TO RETURN TO JERUSALEM

REBUILDING OF TEMPLE BEGINS 536

Edict on Cyrus
Cylinder 536 BC

Zev Radovan

EZEKIEL c. 620-570

TEMPLE COMPLETED 516

DANIEL c. 620-540

**ZERUBBABEL AND JESHUA LEAD THE JEWS
TO FINISH REBUILDING THE TEMPLE** 520-516
ESTHER c. 478

MALACHI c. 465
EZRA SENT TO JUDAH 457
JOEL c. 450

JEHOIACHIN (JECONIAH) 598-597

ZEDEKIAH (MATTANIAH) 597-586

NEHEMIAH GOVERNS JUDAH 444-432
NEHEMIAH IN BABYLON c. 432-430

**JUDAH, THE SOUTHERN KINGDOM, FALLS
TO BABYLON TEMPLE AND JERUSALEM DESTROYED** 586

**GEDALIAH, GOVERNOR
OF JUDAH** 586

Pericles 500-429

Babylon falls to Persia 539

Peloponnesian War between Athens & Sparta 431-404

Darius (Gubaru) the Mede, governor of Babylon 539

Roman Republic established 509

Herodotus 485-424

Buddha, India 550-480

Egypt ruled by the Persians 525-405

Confucius, Chinese philosopher 551-479

NEO-BABYLONIAN
EMPIRE

PERSIAN EMPIRE

Cyrus the Great 559-530

Xerxes I (Ahasuerus) 485-465

Cambyses 529-522

Darius I 522-486

Xerxes I (Ahasuerus) makes
Esther queen c. 478

Artaxerxes 464-424

Nebuchadnezzar II 604-562

600 BC

500 BC

Darius II 423-405

THE IRON AGE

INTER-TESTAMENTAL PERIOD

400 BC   300 BC

Palestine ruled by Egyptian Ptolemies, the Syrian Seleucids, the Maccabeans and the Romans

PTOLEMAIC EGYPT CONTROLS PALESTINE 331-198

Ephesus ruins

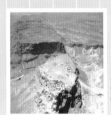
Masada AD 73

Vesuvius Erupts AD 79

Roman Colosseum
built AD 71-80

Zev Radovan

Persia regains control of Egypt 342-332

○ **Alexander the Great conquers Egypt and Palestine, Hellenization begins** 332

First Punic War; Romans control Italy 264-241

○ **Septuagint (scriptures translated into Greek in Alexandria)** c. 255

Second Punic War; Hannibal in Italy 219-201

...PERSIAN EMPIRE

Artaxerxes II 404-359

○ Gauls sack Rome 390

Artaxerxes III 358-337

ALEXANDRIAN EMPIRE

Alexander the Great 336-323

Ptolemy I 323-285

Seleucus I 312-280

Ptolemy II 285-246

PTOLEMIES OF EGYPT

Antiochus I 280-261

Antiochus II 261-247

Ptolemy III 246-221

Ptolemy IV 221-203

Egypt independent from Persia 405-342

○ Alexandrian Empire divided; Ptolemy rules Egypt, Seleucus rules Persia and Syria, Antigonus rules Macedonia and Greece 323

Antiochus III the Great 223-187

400 BC   300 BC

THE IRON AGE

INTER-TESTAMENTAL PERIOD

200 BC   100 BC

Palestine ruled by Egyptian Ptolemies, the Syrian Seleucids, the Maccabeans and the Romans

JESUS BORN IN BETHLEHEM 6-4 BC

○ The Syrian Seleucids begin to rule Palestine 198

Jewish priests on good terms with the Seleucids 180-190   **JOHN THE BAPTIST BORN** 7-5 BC ○

The Seleucid ruler Antiochus IV tries to force Jews to
abandon their law, desecrates the temple 175-163
Judas Maccabeus leads a Jewish revolt against the Seleucids 166-160
Jonathan, brother of Judas Maccabeus continues revolt 160-143

Temple in ○   ○ Hasmoneans take control of the priesthood 152
Jerusalem   Third Punic War; Romans control Greece 149-146
rededicated,   Simon, brother of Judas Maccabeus, governs Judea 142-135
Hanukkah 164   John Hyrcanus I, high priest 134-104

John Hyrcanus I ○   Aristobulus I declares himself ruler of Judea 104-103
becomes ruler of   Alexander Jannaeus succeeds Aristobulus as king 103-76
Judea 129   Sulla dictator of Rome 82-79

Salome Alexander 76-67

Spartacus leads slave revolt 73-71

Aristobulus II 67-63

Pompey conquers Jerusalem for Rome 63 ○

Hyrcanus II, high priest 63-40

Cleopatra VII rules Egypt 51-31

Battle of Phillipi 42 ○
Herod the Great appointed king of Judea 37-4

Battle of Actium, Rome controls Egypt 31 ○
Herod begins refurbishing the Temple 20○

○ Rosetta Stone Tribute to Ptolemy V written in Greek,
Egyptian hieroglyphs and Egyptian demotic 196   Hillel and Shammai are the leading rabbis 30 BC-AD 10

Philo Judaeus of Alexandria 20 BC-AD 50

Dead Sea Scrolls (copies of scriptures) written c. 200 BC-AD 100

Hasmonean dynasty (Jewish Self Rule) 164-63

SELEUCIDS OF SYRIA	Antiochus V Eupator 163-162		ROMAN EMPIRE
	Demetrius I Soter 162-150	Caesar Augustus (Octavian), first Roman Emperor 27 BC-AD 14	
Seleucus IV Philopator 187-175	Alexander Balas 150-145		○Julius Caesar, Crassus and Pompey form the First Triumvirate 60
	Antiochus IV Epiphanes 175-163	Demetrius II 145-138	
		Antiochus VI 145-142	
Ptolemy V 203-181		Antiochus VII Sidetes 138-129	
		Demetrius III 129-125	
		Antiochus VIII Grypus 125-96	
		Antiochus IX Cyzicanus 116-95	

200 BC   100 BC

THE IRON AGE

MATTHEW, LUKE

MARK, JOHN, ACTS, JAMES, GALATIANS, 1 & 2 THESSALONIANS, HEBREWS, 1 & 2 CORINTHIANS, ROMANS, EPHESIANS, PHILEMON, COLOSSIANS, TITUS, PHILLIPIANS, 1 & 2 TIMOTHY, 1 & 2 PETER, JUDE, 1, 2, 3, JOHN, REVELATION

AD 1   AD 50   AD 100 >

New Testament

HEROD ARCHELAUS RULES JUDEA 4 BC-AD 6

HEROD ANTIPAS RULES GALILEE 4 BC-AD 39

JUDEA BECOMES A ROMAN PROVINCE RULED BY A GOVERNOR 6-41, 44-46

○ JESUS AMAZES THE TEACHERS IN THE TEMPLE c. AD 7

CAIAPHAS, HIGH PRIEST 18-36

JESUS BAPTIZED, MINISTRY BEGINS c. 26   PONTIUS PILATE, GOVERNOR OF JUDEA 26-36

CRUCIFIXION, DEATH AND RESURRECTION OF JESUS CHRIST c. 30

RISEN CHRIST SEEN BY MORE THAN 500 PEOPLE, ASCENDS TO HEAVEN c. 30

STEPHEN MARTYRED c. 32 ○

PAUL'S CONVERSION 37

GOSPEL PREACHED TO GENTILES 40 ○

HEROD AGRIPPA I, KING OF JUDEA 41-44

JAMES THE APOSTLE MARTYRED ○ c. 44

PAUL'S FIRST MISSIONARY JOURNEY c. 47-49

COUNCIL OF JERUSALEM c. 49 ○

EARLIEST NEW TESTAMENT BOOKS WRITTEN c. 49

○ JEWS, INCLUDING PRISCILLA AND AQUILA, EXPELLED FROM ROME 49

PAUL'S SECOND MISSIONARY JOURNEY c. 49-51

FELIX, GOVERNOR OF JUDEA 52-57

PAUL'S THIRD MISSIONARY JOURNEY c. 52-57

FESTUS, GOVERNOR OF JUDEA 59-62

○ JAMES, THE BROTHER OF JESUS, MARTYRED 62

○ PETER AND PAUL MARTYRED IN ROME c. 64 or c. 68

○ JERUSALEM CHRISTIANS FLEE RATHER THAN JOIN THE JEWISH REVOLT 66

JEWISH REVOLT 66-73

APOSTLE JOHN EXILED TO PATMOS IN THE AEGEAN SEA
Some scholars believe John's exile was under Domitian's rule (c. 85-96) and others believe it was under Nero's rule (c. 68).

BOOK OF REVELATION WRITTEN c. 90-96 or c. 68-69

○ Qumran destroyed 68

Romans destroy Jewish temple and Jerusalem 70

○ Construction begins on Roman Colosseum 71

Claudius conquers Britain for Rome 43 ○

Philo Judaeus of Alexandria 20 BC-AD 50

Josephus, Jewish historian 37-100

○ Masada falls to Romans 73

Mt. Vesuvius erupts, destroying Pompeii and Herculaneum 79 ○

Dedication of Colosseum 80 ○

Caesar Augustus (Octavian), first Roman Emperor 27 BC-AD 14

Emperor Tiberius 14-37

Emperor Caligula 37-41

Emperor Claudius 41-54

Gallio, proconsul of Achaia 51-52

Emperor Nero 54-68

Rome burns, Nero blames and persecutes Christians 64-68

○ Emperors Galba, Otho, Vitellius 68-69

Emperor Vespasian 69-79

Emperor Titus 79-81

Emperor Domitian (81-96) demands title "Lord and God"

Emperor Nerva 96-98

Emperor Trajan 98-117

AD 1   AD 100 >

THE IRON AGE

Dates listed are approximate. Contributor: Timothy Paul Jones, Ed.D.
Thanks to: Alfred J. Hoerth, Director of Archaeology emeritus, Wheaton College; Gary M. Burge, Ph.D., Professor of New Testament, Wheaton College; John Monson, Ph.D.; Richard Schultz, Ph.D.

How to Study
the Bible

Basic Principles of Bible Study

Why Study the Bible?

Inductive Bible Study

Ways to Study

Tools for Bible Study

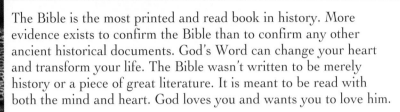

WHY STUDY THE BIBLE?

The Bible is the most printed and read book in history. More evidence exists to confirm the Bible than to confirm any other ancient historical documents. God's Word can change your heart and transform your life. The Bible wasn't written to be merely history or a piece of great literature. It is meant to be read with both the mind and heart. God loves you and wants you to love him.

Reasons to Study with Your Mind and Heart

To know God — God created the heaven and the earth and everyone in it. (Genesis 1-3)

To enjoy and love God — Meditate on God's character, principles, and promises. Rejoice in his love, care, and forgiveness. (Psalm 119:12-18, 160-162; 1 Timothy 6:17)

To know God's Word — The Scriptures were inspired by God. They teach us the truth and show us what is wrong in our lives. They straighten us out. (2 Timothy 3:16)

To understand the Word — Jesus is called the Word because he is the ultimate communication from God. He existed from the beginning with God, he is God, and he created everything. He said that those who have seen him have seen the Father. (John 1:1-3; 10:30; 12:44, 45; 14:7-9)

To learn direction in life — The Bible shows us what to do. (Psalm 119:11)

To find comfort and hope — The Scriptures give us encouragement. (Romans 15:4)

To let God expose our innermost thoughts and desires — His Word helps us see ourselves as we really are and convicts us of sin so that we repent and change. (Hebrews 4:12-16)

To become pure and holy — Jesus prayed this for all believers that they would be set apart for God and his holy purposes. (John 17:17-23)

To obey the Great Commandment — The more we know God, the more we can love him. The Great Commandment is to love God with all of our being and our neighbor as ourselves (Mark 12:29-31). And Jesus gave us a new commandment to love one another (John 13:34-35).

HOW TO BEGIN STUDYING THE BIBLE

Plan a Study Time
Decide on a quiet time and place to study God's Word and make it a daily habit, like eating. Some people get up early to spend time with God. Others study during the day or evening.

Pray
Ask God to help you understand his Word. Pray using your own words or something like this: "Lord, thank you for the Bible so that we will know who you are and what you want for our lives. Please help me understand it and do what you want me to do."

Read and Re-read It
The Bible is the most important letter you can ever receive—a message from the God of the universe who made you, loves you, and wants to communicate with you. Open your "love letter" every day. Re-read each chapter and verse several times.

Know the Author
Read Genesis to learn about God who created the world. All Scripture is inspired by God. God actually visited Earth in the form of man—the man Christ Jesus. Jesus said, "I and my Father are one." Read the Gospel of John to learn about God's plan for you.

Take Notes
Write notes about what you read. Use a specific notebook or "spiritual journal" especially for Bible study. The three questions of "Inductive Bible Study" will help you look at the facts and discover how they apply to you. You might want to underline key verses or write notes in the margin of your Bible.

Make the Bible Your Authority
Accept and believe that what the Bible says is true. You may not understand everything in the Bible, but obey and apply what you do understand.

Find a Group
"As iron sharpens iron, so one person sharpens another" (Proverbs 27:17). God gave his Word to his people. When you share what you are learning with other fellow believers, God will do amazing things. It will also help you to be accountable to someone.

BASIC PRINCIPLES OF BIBLE STUDY

GENESIS

Who: Moses
What: The Beginnings
Where: Egypt and Canaan
When: c. 1450 BC–1400 BC
Why: To demonstrate that God is sovereign and loves his creation.

Outline (Chapter)
- Creation, Fall, and Flood (1-11)
- Abraham (11-25)
- Isaac and Jacob (25-36)
- Joseph (37-50)

Key Verse: *I will establish my covenant as an everlasting covenant between me and you and your descendants after you for the generations to come, to be your God and the God of your descendants after you.* (Genesis 17:7)

JOHN

Who: John (The Beloved Disciple)
What: Gospel
Where: Asia Minor
When: c. AD 85–AD 95
Why: To show Jesus as the Son of God, the Word made flesh, who provides eternal life for all who believe in him.

Outline (Chapter)
- Introduction (1)
- Ministry of Christ (2-12)
- Private Ministry (13-17)
- Death and Resurrection (18-21)

Key Verse: *For God so loved the world, that he gave his only begotten Son, that whosoever believeth in him should not perish, but have everlasting life.* (John 3:16)

Look for God's Over-All Plan

The Old Testament reveals God's loving plan of salvation, from Creation to prophecies of the future Messiah (the Savior).

The New Testament reveals God's salvation of sinful man by the suffering, death and resurrection of the Messiah, Jesus Christ, and reveals the everlasting Kingdom of God.

God inspired 40 people over a period of 1600 years to write the 66 books of the Bible.

Find the Background of the Books (Five W's and One H)

Find out who wrote the books and the reason for, or theme of, the books. Ask "Who, What, Where, When, Why, and How?" Usually this information is in the first chapter or in the introduction to the book.

Read Verses in Context

Read the surrounding chapters and the verses *before* and *after* the verse you are studying. Get the whole picture. Don't study verses out of context. Look at the outline of the book.

Whole Message of God's Word

Take the whole Bible as God's Word. Don't just concentrate on one verse or one idea. See if the teaching is explained more fully in other parts of the Bible. Look at the small cross references in your Bible to help you find other verses on the same subject. For example, look at the cross references and the verses around John 3:16.

Sample page of John 3:12-18 from a Bible with cross references.

12 If I have told you earthly things, and ye believe not, how shall ye believe, if I tell you of heavenly things?

13 And *no man hath ascended up to heaven, but *he that came down from heaven, *even *the Son of man which is in heaven.

14 And as Moses lifted up the serpent in the wilderness, even so must the Son of man *be lifted up.

15 That whosoever believeth *in him should not perish, but have eternal life.

Cross references

13 *a* Pr 30:4;
Deu 30:12;
Ac 2:34
b Jn 3:31;
6:38
c Mt 8:20

14 *a* Jn 8:28;
12:34

15 *a* Jn 20:31;
1 Jn 5:11

16 For God so *loved the world, that he *gave his *only begotten Son, that whosoever *believeth in him should not perish, but have everlasting life.

17. For God *sent not his Son into the world *to condemn the world; but that the world through him might be saved.

18 *He that believeth on him is not condemned: but he that believeth not is condemned already, because he hath not believed in the name of the only begotten Son of God.

16 *a* Ro 5:8;
Eph 2:4; 1 Jn
4:10　　*b* Ro
8:32; 1 Jn 4:9
c Jn 1:18; 3:18
d Jn 3:36;
6:40

17 *a* Jn 3:54;
5:36; 6:29;
20:21 *b* Jn
8:15; 12:47;
1 Jn 4:14

18 *a* Mk 6:16;
Jn 5:24 *b* Jn
1:18; 1 Jn 4:9

BASIC PRINCIPLES OF BIBLE STUDY

Discover the Intended Meaning

As you read the Bible, look for the author's intended meaning. What did the author want to say? What did it mean in that culture? What does it mean now? What are the main ideas? If you have questions, write them down, pray for insight, and discuss your ideas with others.

Learn the History and Geography

Use a time line to learn about the history of the Bible. Use maps to learn about the geography of where the events took place.

Figurative Language

Figures of speech are word pictures that help us understand a truth. "Thy Word is a lamp unto my feet, and a light unto my path" is a metaphor that helps us picture the Bible enlightening our minds and actions and giving us direction. "As the deer pants for the water brooks, so pants my soul for you, O God" is a simile that compares ideas with the words "like" or "as." Similes occur over 175 times in the Psalms. Jesus used personification when he said if the people did not declare the mighty works they had seen God do, the stones would cry out in praise. Hyperbole (exaggeration) is found in Matthew 5:29-30.

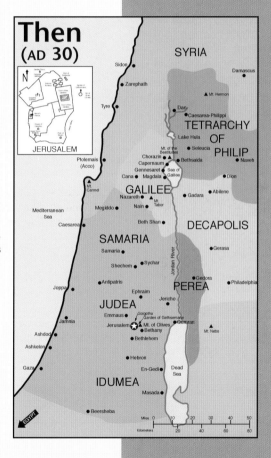

Forms of Literature

The Bible contains various forms of literature: History, Narrative, Poetry, Wisdom, Prophecy, Parables and Letters. Recognizing each form will help you interpret the meaning. For example, parables explain a spiritual truth by means of a story or analogy. The parable of the Prodigal Son does not refer to a specific historical person but teaches that God is a loving father who joyfully welcomes back prodigal or rebellious children who later repent and return to him.

INDUCTIVE BIBLE STUDY

What does it say?
What does it mean?
How does it apply to me?

1. How can I find out for myself what the Bible says?
Read it and re-read the Bible passage using the "Basic Principles of Study". Read silently some times and read aloud other times. Don't start by reading what others have concluded about the Bible. Inductive reasoning moves from specific examples to general conclusions. Deductive reasoning moves from general examples to specific conclusions.

2. How can I know what the Bible means?
After reading the facts, you can summarize them. Don't jump to conclusions too fast. Read the passage several times and pray for wisdom. You will learn more and remember more if you discover what the Scriptures say yourself. Look at cross references (other verses in Scripture that relate to the verses you read).

3. How can I apply what the Bible says to myself?
The goal of Bible study is a transformed life and a deep relationship with God. Sometimes in Scripture, you will see a command to obey, an example to follow, a lesson to learn, or a sin to confess. Apply that to your life.
Other times, you will want to claim a promise, pray a prayer, forgive someone, or ask forgiveness. Listen to the "still small voice" of God. God says, "Be still and know that I am God." As you listen and respond to God, you will be amazed at the results in your life as your relationship with him deepens.
(1 Kings 19:12, Psalm 46:10)

Resources: Inexpensive *Life Journals* for all ages are available at New Hope Resources at 1-877-755-9555 http://resources.enewhope.org/store/ Personalized Bibles (with your own name inserted into the verses) are available at Personal Promise Bible at 1-866-YOUR BIBLE. Source: Pamphlet. www.personalpromisebible.com/

SOME BASIC BIBLE PASSAGES TO STUDY

Start with these Books: ❏ Genesis ❏ John

Short Books: ❏ 1 John ❏ 1 Thessalonians

Book Study: 11 More Books to Study
  ❏ Mark, Matthew, or Luke ❏ Acts ❏ Galatians ❏ Ephesians
  ❏ Philippians ❏ Colossians ❏ 2 Thessalonians ❏ 1 Timothy
  ❏ 2 Timothy ❏ Psalms ❏ Proverbs

Chapter Study: 11 Key Chapters
  ❏ John 1, 3, 4 ❏ John 14, 15, 16, 17
  ❏ Romans 6, 8, 12 ❏ Ephesians 5

Passage Study: 7 Key Passages
  ❏ The Fall of Man—Genesis 3
  ❏ The Ten Commandments—Exodus 20:1-17
  ❏ The Prophecy of the Coming Messiah—Isaiah 53
  ❏ The Beatitudes—Matthew 5:1-11
  ❏ The Sermon on the Mount—Matthew 5-7
  ❏ Two Great Commandments—Matthew 22:36-40
  ❏ The Prodigal Son—Luke 15:11-32

Verse Study: 17 Key Verses to Memorize
  ❏ Genesis 1:1 ❏ Proverbs 3:5, 6 ❏ John 3:16 ❏ John 1:9, 12
  ❏ Romans 3:23 ❏ Romans 6:23 ❏ Romans 5:8 ❏ Romans 10:9
  ❏ Ephesians 2:8, 9 ❏ Acts 16:30, 31 ❏ Philippians 4:6, 7
  ❏ Psalm 119:11

WAYS TO STUDY

Bible Studies
Study alone or with a partner. Small groups and home study groups can help you ask questions and share insights. Attend a Sunday School class or Bible Study at a Bible-teaching church.

Psalms and Proverbs
Read five Psalms and one chapter of Proverbs each day. (You'll read the 150 Psalms and 31 chapters of Proverbs in a month.)

Overview of the Bible
Read through the Bible in one year (about three chapters a day). One-Year Bibles and calendars give daily passages to read.

Listen to Learn
Listen to tapes of the Bible, radio programs that teach the Bible, and sermons that teach from the Bible. Taking notes is helpful.

Discuss the Bible With Others
Share what you've learned with others. Their questions will challenge you to pray and study more to find the answers.

Good Books on Bible Study
Discipleship Journal's Best Bible Study Methods, Munro & Couchman, NavPress, 2002.
How to Study Your Bible, Kay Arthur, Harvest House, 2001.
How to Study The Bible, R. A. Torrey, Whitaker House, 1986.
How to Study The Bible and Enjoy It, Skip Heitzig, Tyndale House, 2002
Rick Warren's Bible Study Methods, Rick Warren, Zondervan, 2006.
How to Get the Most from God's Word, John MacArthur, Jr., Word Publishing
How to Read the Bible For All It's Worth, Fee and Stuart, Zondervan, 1982
Bible Study Made Easy, Mark Water, Hendrickson Publishers, 1992

Other Materials for Bible Study
How We Got the Bible chart and pamphlet, Rose Publishing
50 Proofs for the Bible: OT and *NT* pamphlet, Rose Publishing
100 Prophecies Fulfilled by Jesus chart and pamphlet, Rose Publishing

TOOLS FOR BIBLE STUDY

1. Study Bibles
A study Bible will help you a great deal. Study Bibles contain explanations, introductions, outlines, cross references and study notes. A good study Bible has a concordance, maps, and a topical index. Ask your pastor to recommend one.

2. Concordances
A concordance helps you look up any word in the Bible. It gives an alphabetical listing of key words, names, and topics, plus a list of verses that contain that word.

3. Bible Software
Bible concordances and other references are available on both desktop and hand held software. Enter a word or reference to quickly find and print out Bible verses in various versions. Complete Bible libraries and study Bibles are available on computer software.

4. Bible Dictionaries
Look up words you don't understand, such as "grace," "redemption," or "faith." Expository dictionaries give you more detailed meanings and explanations.

5. Bible Atlases, Maps, and Time Lines
On a map, locate *where* Bible events took place. Daniel was in Babylon. Babylon ruins are south of Baghdad today. On a time line, locate *when* Bible events took place. During the fierce Assyrian Kingdom, around 781 BC, Jonah went to Nineveh to warn the people to repent.

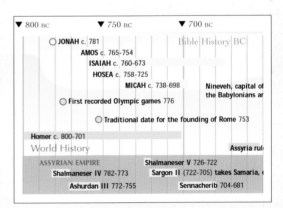

6. Bible Commentaries and Handbooks
First, study the Bible yourself. See what it means and how it applies to you. List questions you have. Later, you can read to see how Bible scholars explain it.

7. Special Bibles
Topical Bibles organize Scripture in special areas of interest, such as Salvation, Marriage, or Prayer. **Interlinear Bibles** compare original language (Hebrew or Greek) to modern language. **Large-print Bibles** are easy to read and helpful for many people.

DIGGING DEEPER:

Bible study is important to our growth as followers of Jesus. Jesus compares reading the Bible with a seed being planted in good soil. The seed planted in good soil represents those with an honest and good heart, who hear the word, apply it, and with patience, produce a crop or fruit. Read Luke 8:4-15.

Selection

What do I study?

1. Pray
"Open my eyes that I may see wonderful things in your law." (Psalm 119:18)

2. Become Familiar with the Bible
- The Old Testament was written before Jesus' birth and tells about the people of Israel and anticipates the coming of Jesus the Messiah. The New Testament was written about Jesus' birth, life, ministry, death and resurrection and the years that followed as Christianity spread.
- Know the type of book you are reading such as Law, Prophet, History, Poetry, and so on. This can be found in the introduction to a Study Bible.
- Memorize the order of the Books of the Bible.
- Learn how to read the references:
  For example: 2 Timothy 3:16
  2 = Second letter or book
  Timothy = Name of letter or book
  3: = chapter
  :16 = verse

3. Select the Passage
Determine where the passage begins and ends.

4. Select a Version
Decide on a translation such as the King James Version (KJV), the New International Version (NIV), the New Living Translation (NLT), the New King James Version (NKJV), or the New American Standard Bible Update (NASBM).

5. Remember the Four "Do-Nots"
- Do not "proof text" (take verses out of context).
- Do not be too literal (see Matthew 5:29, 30).
- Do not ignore the Bible's cultural, historical, and literary background.
- Do not read your own ideas into the Scriptures.

Observation

What do I see?

1. Make Use of Tools
Study Bibles, commentaries, concordances, Bible dictionaries, Bible encyclopedias, interlinear Bible (Greek and Hebrew to English), Bible handbooks, and Bible atlases, time lines, and topical Bibles.

2. Observe the Text
- Do word studies. Observe words or expressions. Notice synonyms (words that have similar meanings) and antonyms (words that have opposite meanings). Pay attention to reoccurring words.
- Who are the people in the passage?
- What are the important ideas in the passage?
- Where are the places in the story?
- Pay attention to timespans.
- What is the literary genre (form), such as Narrative (story), Epic, Priestly Writings, Law, Liturgy, Poetry, Lament, Teaching, Prophecy, Gospel, Parable, Epistle (letter), or Apocalyptic literature?

3. Observe the Context
- What is the immediate context? What comes before and after the text?
- Who is talking? Who is listening?

4. Observe the Historical Setting
- When was this passage written?
- Where was this passage originally written?
- Who is the author? What is his occupation? What is his personality? Where is he from?
- Who is the original audience? To what nation do they belong? What is their history? Where do they live? Where are they from?
- What is the original purpose for this writing?
- Refer to maps, time lines, and other historical documents for more about the historical, sociological, and geographical setting.

IN-DEPTH BIBLE STUDY

Interpretation

Life Application

What does it mean?

1. The Language Question
- What is the meaning of each word?
- What is the meaning in the original language (Hebrew or Greek)?
- How are significant words used elsewhere in scripture?
- How does the genre affect the text?
- What is the form (such as the structure of the Abraham story in Genesis 11-25)?
- What is the sentence structure?
- Why are particular words used?
- Compare this passage to other versions of the Bible.

2. The Historical Question
- How does the historical situation affect this text?
- How does the sociological situation affect this text?
- How does the geographical situation affect this text?

3. The Theological Question
- What truths are taught about the nature of God?
- What does this passage tell us about human nature?
- Does this passage have anything to say about sin?
- Does this passage teach truths about redemption and salvation?
- What does this passage have to say about the church and/or the Christian life?

4. The Tactical Question
- How does each paragraph fit into the author's reason for writing?

How does this apply?

1. The Contemporary Question
- How do we apply what the author has said to the assumptions, values, and goals of our lives and society?
- What are the principles found in this passage that apply to the contemporary situation?
- How is God's redemption illustrated by this passage?
- Is there anything this passage has to say about certain social issues, such as racism, justice, poverty, or money?

2. The Personal Question
- How do we relate what the author says to our personalities?
- How do we relate this passage to our personal needs?
- How does this passage impact our families and close friends?
- What does this passage say about our moral decisions?
- How does the text affect our personal goals?
- How do these verses or principles apply to the Church as a body?

3. The Final Question
- What am I going to do about what I have learned?
- What personal goals am I going to set in my life to implement the truths found in this passage?
- How does this passage impact my relationship with God?

4. Pray About What You Learned
- Pray for God's strength to help you to grow through your study.

BIBLE REFERENCE LIBRARY

A **Study Bible** will bring out the significance of God's Word. In addition, you will want to build a **Reference Library**. Check off each category as your library grows.

References	*Publishers*

Concordance (Locates all the occurrences of a word.)

Strong's Exhaustive	Thomas Nelson Publishers
NAS Exhaustive	Broadman & Holman Publishers
NIV Exhaustive	Zondervan Publishers

Bible Software (Concordance, Libraries, Bibles, Maps)

Scholars Library Series X (PC and Mac)	Logos Bible Software
BibleWorks	BibleWorks, LLC
PC Study Bible (PC)	BibleSoft
QuickVerse (PC and PDA)	QuickVerse
Accordance (Macintosh)	OakSoft
Then & Now Bible Maps PowerPoint®	Rose Publishing

Bible Dictionary (Defines Scripture words; gives some background)

Holman Bible Dictionary	Broadman & Holman
New Illustrated Bible Dictionary	Nelson
Dictionary of the Bible	Eerdmans
New Unger's Dictionary	Moody Press
Zondervan Pictorial	Zondervan

Bible Atlas and Time Lines (Geography maps; history time lines.)

Atlas of Bible Lands	Broadman & Holman
NIV Atlas of the Bible	Zondervan
Moody Bible Atlas	Moody
Deluxe Then & Now Bible Maps book	Rose Publishing
Bible and Christian History Time Lines book	Rose Publishing
Bible Time Line pamphlet	Rose Publishing

Commentary (Written by scholars with years of study; explanations)

One Volume: *Wycliffe Bible Commentary*	Moody
Matthew Henry's Commentary	Zondervan
New Bible Commentary	Eerdman
Two Volume: *Zondervan Commentary*	Zondervan
Bible Knowledge Commentary	Nelson
Bible Exposition Commentary	Victor Books

Bible Handbook (Overview; background; customs and history)

New Unger's Bible Handbook	Moody
Holman Bible Handbook	Broadman & Holman
Halley's Bible Handbook	Zondervan

Topical Bible (Organizes Scripture in special areas of interest)

Nave's Topical Bible	Hendrickson Publishers
Topical Analysis of the Bible	Baker Book House Company

Special thanks to consultants Bill Reynolds ("Mr. Bible"), Dave Wilke, Carleen Shrag, Dr. Robert Cubillos, Dr. Peter Loizeaux, Carolyn Loizeaux, Dan Mahaffie, and Delores Withers.

Then & Now
Bible Maps

Ancient Empires & Kingdoms

The Middle East

United & Divided Kingdoms

The Holy Land

Paul's Journeys

The Middle East: Then (Bible Times) and Now (Modern Times)

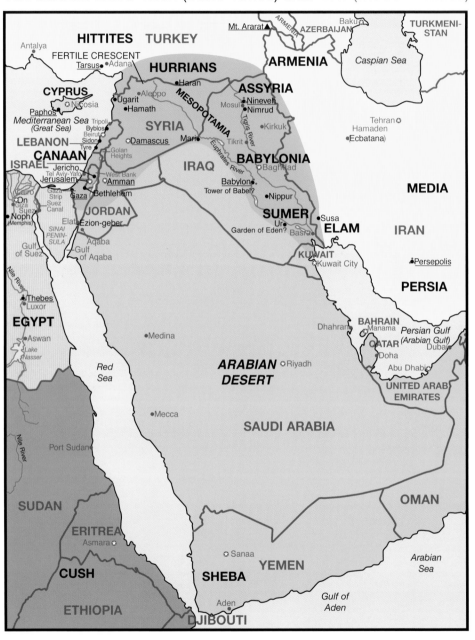

Mt. Ararat▲

TURKEY
HITTITES
Antalya
FERTILE CRESCENT
Tarsus● ●Adana
HURRIANS
CYPRUS
●Aleppo
Byblos
○Nicosia
Paphos○
Mediterranean Sea
(Great Sea)
Tripoli
●Ugarit
●Hamath
SYRIA
MESOPOTAMIA
Beirut
LEBANON
Sidon
Tyre
Golan
Heights
CANAAN
ISRAEL
Jericho
Tel Aviv-Yafo
Jerusalem○
West Bank
●Damascus
Mari●
IRAQ
Cairo
Giza
On
○Amman
Bethlehem
Gaza
Strip
Gaza
Suez
Canal
Noph
(Memphis)
Suez○
JORDAN
Elat
Ezion-geber
Gulf
of Suez
SINAI
PENIN-
SULA
Aqaba
Gulf
of Aqaba

ARMENIA
ARMENIA
AZERBAIJAN
Baku
TURKMENI-STAN
Caspian Sea
ASSYRIA
●Haran
Mosul
●Nineveh
●Nimrud
Tigris River
●Kirkuk
Tikrit ●
Euphrates River
BABYLONIA
Baghdad○
Babylon●
Tower of Babel?
●Nippur
SUMER
Ur●
Garden of Eden?
Basra
Susa
●
ELAM
KUWAIT
○Kuwait City
Tehran○
Hamaden
●Ecbatana)
MEDIA
▲Persepolis
IRAN
PERSIA

Nile River
▲Thebes
●Luxor
EGYPT
●Aswan
Lake
Nasser
●Medina
Red
Sea
●Mecca
Nile River
Port Sudan
**ARABIAN
DESERT**
○Riyadh
SAUDI ARABIA
Dhahran
BAHRAIN
Manama
QATAR
○Doha
Persian Gulf
(Arabian Gulf)
Dubai
Abu Dhabi
**UNITED ARAB
EMIRATES**
OMAN

SUDAN
ERITREA
Asmara○
CUSH
ETHIOPIA
○Sanaa
●Mecca
●Sanaa
SHEBA
YEMEN
Aden●
Gulf of
Aden
Arabian
Sea
DJIBOUTI

0 100 200 300 400 500
miles
km
0 100 200 300 400 500 600 700 800

● City or Town
∴ Ancient Ruins/Sites
▲ Mountain
✪ Modern Capital Cities

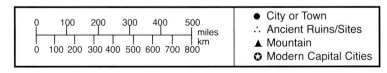

Ancient cities and sites that have the same name today are <u>underlined in red</u>.

The Holy Land: Then (1300 BC – Twelve Tribes) and Now (Modern Times)

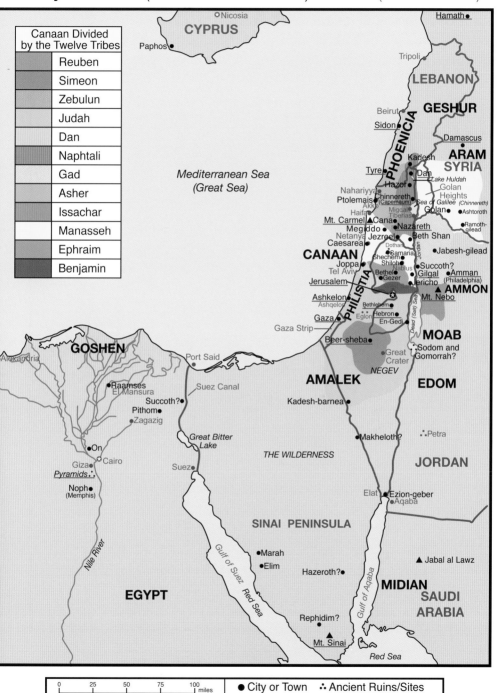

Canaan Divided by the Twelve Tribes	
	Reuben
	Simeon
	Zebulun
	Judah
	Dan
	Naphtali
	Gad
	Asher
	Issachar
	Manasseh
	Ephraim
	Benjamin

CYPRUS
Nicosia
Paphos
Hamath
Tripoli
LEBANON
GESHUR
Beirut
Sidon
Damascus
PHOENICIA
Kadesh
ARAM
Tyre
Dan
SYRIA
Lake Huldah
Hazor
Golan
Heights
Nahariyya
Chinnereth
Ptolemais
(Capernaum)
Sea of Galilee (Chinnereth)
Golan
Ashtoroth
AKKO
Migdal
Haifa
Tiberias
Mt. Carmel
Cana
Nazareth
Ramoth-gilead
Megiddo
Jezreel
Beth Shan
Netanya
Dothan
Caesarea
CANAAN
Samaria
Jabesh-gilead
Shechem
Joppa
Shiloh
Succoth?
Nablus
Bethel
Gilgal
Amman
Jerusalem
Gezer
Jericho
(Philadelphia)
Ashkelon
Bethlehem
Mt. Nebo
AMMON
Ashqelon
PHILISTIA
Hebron
Gaza
Eglon
En-Gedi
Gaza Strip
Dead (Salt) Sea
MOAB
Beer-sheba
Sodom and
Great
Gomorrah?
Crater
NEGEV
EDOM
AMALEK
Mediterranean Sea
(Great Sea)

GOSHEN
Alexandria
Port Said
Raamses
El Mansura
Suez Canal
Succoth?
Kadesh-barnea
Pithom
Zagazig
Great Bitter
Lake
THE WILDERNESS
Makheloth?
Petra
On
Suez
Giza
Cairo
Pyramids
JORDAN
Noph
(Memphis)
Elat
Ezion-geber
Aqaba
SINAI PENINSULA
Nile River
Marah
Jabal al Lawz
Elim
Gulf of Suez
Red Sea
Hazeroth?
Gulf of Aqaba
MIDIAN
EGYPT
SAUDI
ARABIA
Rephidim?
Mt. Sinai
Red Sea

0	25	50	75	100	
					miles
0	25	50	75	100	125	150	km

● City or Town   ∴ Ancient Ruins/Sites
▲ Mountain   ✪ Modern Capital Cities

Ancient cities and sites that have the same name today are underlined in red.

EMPIRES & KINGDOMS: Assyrian Empire Then and Now

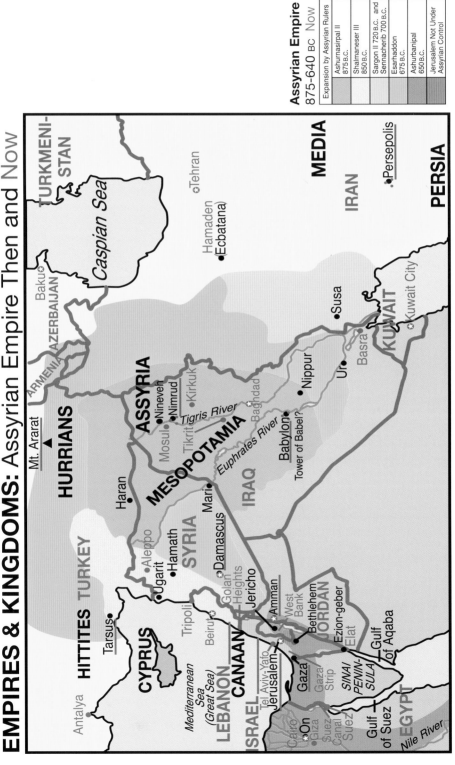

Assyrian Empire
875–640 BC Now

Expansion by Assyrian Rulers

	Ashurnasirpal II 875 B.C.
	Shalmaneser III 850 B.C.
	Sargon II 720 B.C. and Sennacherib 700 B.C.
	Esarhaddon 675 B.C.
	Ashurbanipal 650 B.C.
	Jerusalem Not Under Assyrian Control

Ancient cities and sites that have the same name today are underlined in red.

EMPIRES & KINGDOMS: Babylonian Kingdom Then and Now

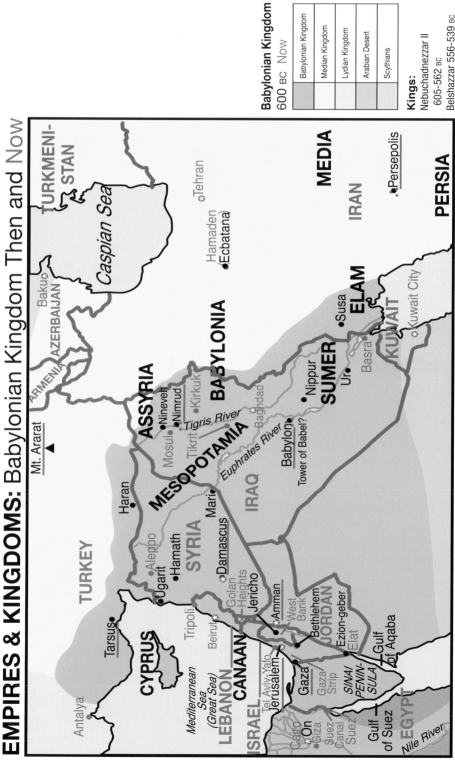

Babylonian Kingdom
600 BC   Now

	Babylonian Kingdom
	Median Kingdom
	Lydian Kingdom
	Arabian Desert
	Scythians

Kings:
Nebuchadnezzar II
605-562 BC
Belshazzar 556-539 BC

TURKMENI-STAN

MEDIA

IRAN

PERSIA

•Persepolis

Caspian Sea

Baku○
AZERBAIJAN

○Tehran

Hamaden
•(Ecbatana)

ELAM

•Susa

KUWAIT

☼Kuwait City

Ur•

Basra○

SUMER

•Nippur

Baghdad○

BABYLONIA

•Kirkuk

ARMENIA

Mt. Ararat
▲

ASSYRIA

Nineveh•
Nimrud•

Mosul○

Tikrit

Tigris River

Babylon•
Tower of Babel?

Euphrates River

IRAQ

MESOPOTAMIA

Mari•

Haran
•

SYRIA

Aleppo
•Hamath

Ugarit•

Damascus○

Golan
Heights

Jericho•

TURKEY

Antalya

Tarsus•

CYPRUS

*Mediterranean
Sea
(Great Sea)*

Tripoli
Beirut•

LEBANON

CANAAN

ISRAEL

Tel Aviv-Yafo
Jerusalem☆

Amman•

West
Bank

Bethlehem

JORDAN

Ezion-geber
Elat

Gulf
of Aqaba

Gaza
Gaza
Strip

SINAI
PENIN-
SULA

On•

Cairo○
•Giza

Suez
Canal
Suez

Gulf
of Suez

Nile River

EGYPT

Ancient cities and sites that have the same name today are underlined in red.

EMPIRES & KINGDOMS: Persian Empire Then and Now

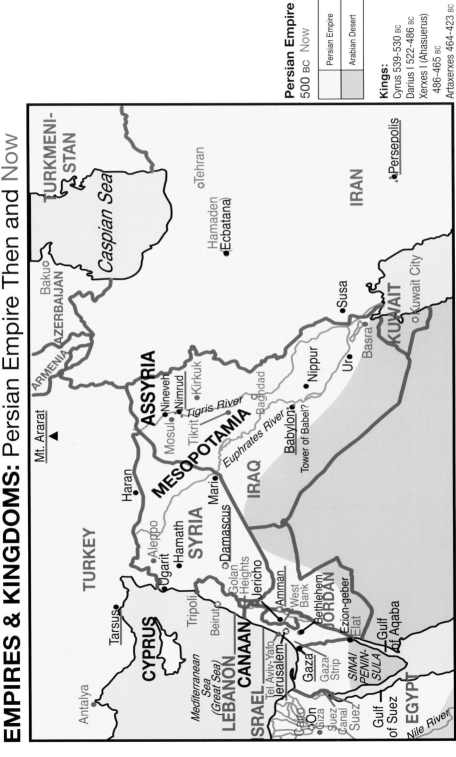

Persian Empire
500 BC Now

	Persian Empire
	Arabian Desert

Kings:
Cyrus 539-530 BC
Darius I 522-486 BC
Xerxes I (Ahasuerus) 486-465 BC
Artaxerxes 464-423 BC

TURKMENI-STAN

Caspian Sea

Baku
AZERBAIJAN
ARMENIA
Mt. Ararat

Tehran

Hamaden (Ecbatana)

IRAN

Persepolis

ASSYRIA
Nineveh
Mosul Nimrud
Tikrit Kirkuk
Tigris River

Haran

MESOPOTAMIA
Mari
Baghdad
Euphrates River
Babylon
Tower of Babel?
IRAQ

Nippur

Ur

Susa

Basra

KUWAIT
Kuwait City

TURKEY

Aleppo
Ugarit Hamath
SYRIA
Damascus
Golan Heights
Jericho
Amman
West Bank
Bethlehem
JORDAN
Ezion-geber
Elat
Gulf of Aqaba

Tarsus

CYPRUS

Antalya

Mediterranean Sea (Great Sea)
Tripoli
Beirut
LEBANON
CANAAN
ISRAEL
Tel Aviv-Yafo
Jerusalem
Gaza
Gaza Strip
SINAI PENIN-SULA

Cairo
On
Giza
Suez Canal
Suez
Gulf of Suez
EGYPT
Nile River

Ancient cities and sites that have the same name today are underlined in red.

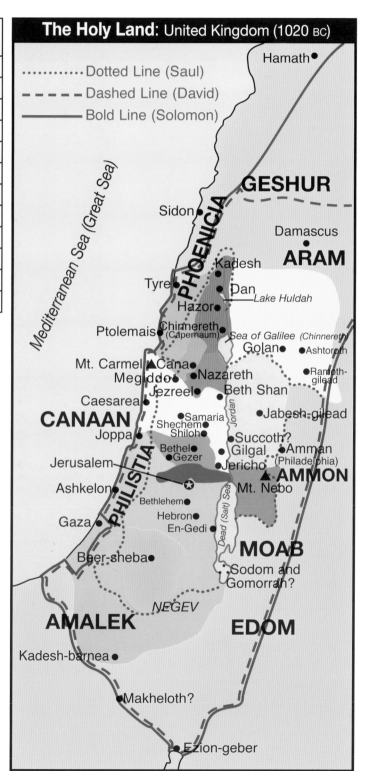

Canaan Divided by the Twelve Tribes	
	Reuben
	Simeon
	Zebulun
	Judah
	Dan
	Naphtali
	Gad
	Asher
	Issachar
	Manasseh
	Ephraim
	Benjamin

The Holy Land: United Kingdom (1020 BC)

············ Dotted Line (Saul)
– – – – Dashed Line (David)
——— Bold Line (Solomon)

Hamath

Mediterranean Sea (Great Sea)

GESHUR

Sidon
PHOENICIA

Damascus
ARAM

Kadesh
Tyre
Dan
Lake Huldah
Hazor
Ptolemais
Chinnereth
(Capernaum)
Sea of Galilee (Chinnereth)
Golan
Ashtoroth
Mt. Carmel Cana
Megiddo Nazareth
Ramoth-gilead
Jezreel
Beth Shan
Caesarea
CANAAN
Samaria
Shechem
Jabesh-gilead
Joppa
Shiloh
Succoth?
Bethel
Gilgal
Amman
Gezer
Jericho
(Philadelphia)
Jerusalem
PHILISTIA
AMMON
Ashkelon
Mt. Nebo
Bethlehem
Gaza
Hebron
En-Gedi
Beer-sheba
MOAB
Sodom and Gomorrah?
NEGEV
AMALEK
EDOM
Kadesh-barnea
Makheloth?
Ezion-geber

Jordan

Dead (Salt) Sea

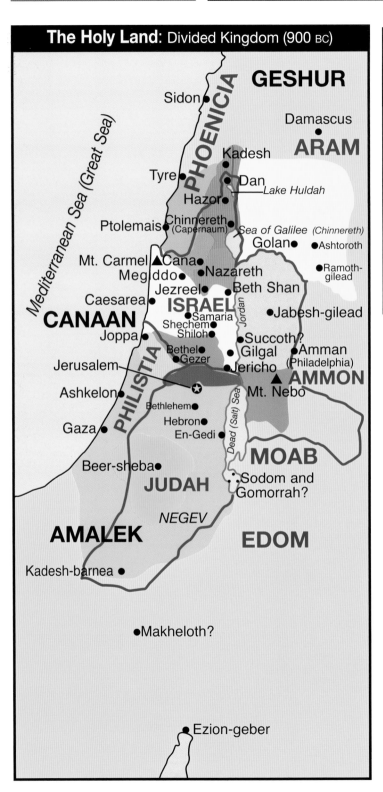

The Holy Land: Divided Kingdom (900 BC)

Canaan Divided by the Twelve Tribes	
	Reuben
	Simeon
	Zebulun
	Judah
	Dan
	Naphtali
	Gad
	Asher
	Issachar
	Manasseh
	Ephraim
	Benjamin

GESHUR

Sidon

PHOENICIA

Damascus

Kadesh

ARAM

Tyre

Dan
Lake Huldah

Hazor

Mediterranean Sea (Great Sea)

Ptolemais
Chinnereth
(Capernaum)
Sea of Galilee (Chinnereth)

Golan
Ashtoroth

Mt. Carmel ▲Cana
Nazareth
Ramoth-gilead

Megiddo
Jezreel
Beth Shan

Caesarea

ISRAEL

Jabesh-gilead

CANAAN

Samaria
Shechem
Shiloh

Joppa

Bethel
Gezer

Succoth?

Gilgal

Jericho

Amman
(Philadelphia)

Jerusalem

✪

▲ AMMON

Ashkelon

PHILISTIA

Mt. Nebo

Bethlehem

Dead (Salt) Sea

Jordan

Gaza

Hebron
En-Gedi

MOAB

Beer-sheba

JUDAH

Sodom and Gomorrah?

NEGEV

AMALEK

EDOM

Kadesh-barnea

•Makheloth?

•Ezion-geber

The Holy Land: Then (New Testament Times AD 1–70) and Now (Modern Times)

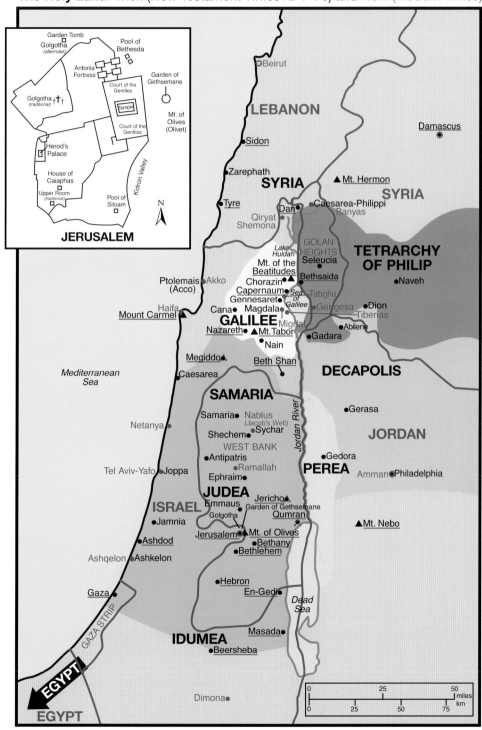

Ancient cities and sites that have the same name today are underlined in red.

PLACES OF JESUS' MINISTRY: Then (AD 26–30) and No

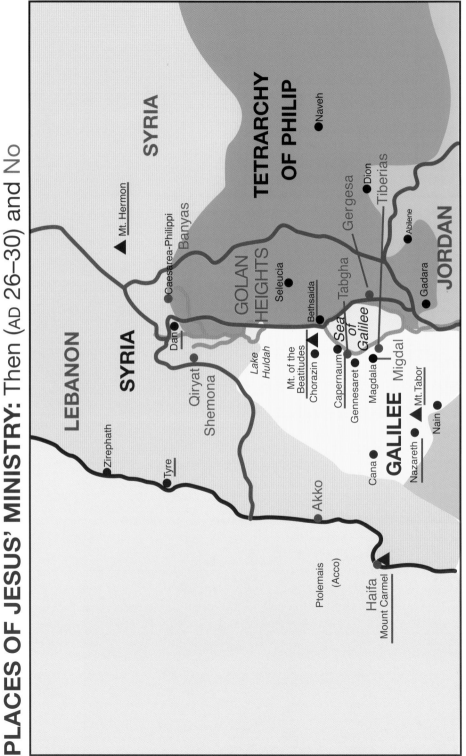

Ancient cities and sites that have the same name today are underlined in red.

PLACES OF JESUS' MINISTRY: Then (AD 26–30) and Now

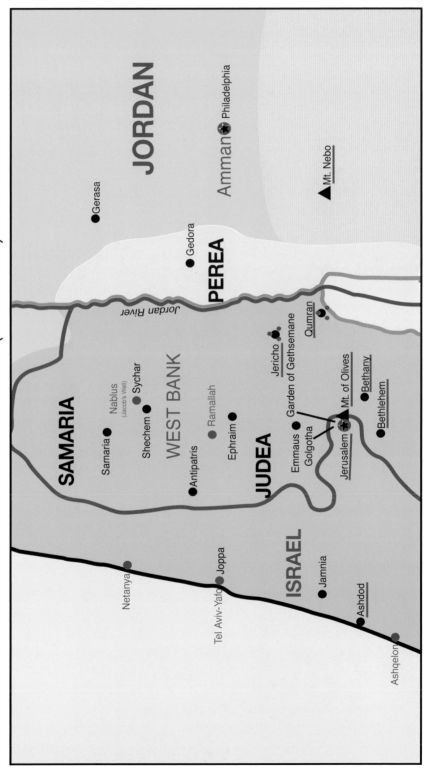

Ancient cities and sites that have the same name today are underlined in red.

PAUL'S JOURNEYS:
Then (AD 47–62) and Now (Modern Times)

Ancient cities and sites that have the same name today are underlined in red.

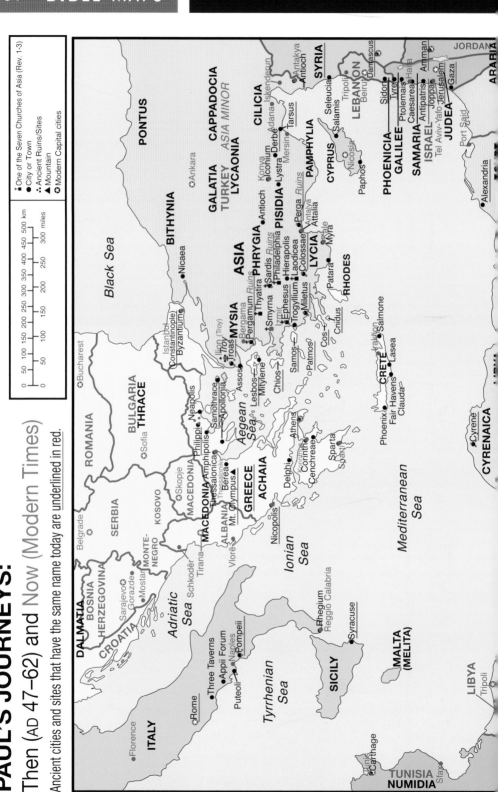

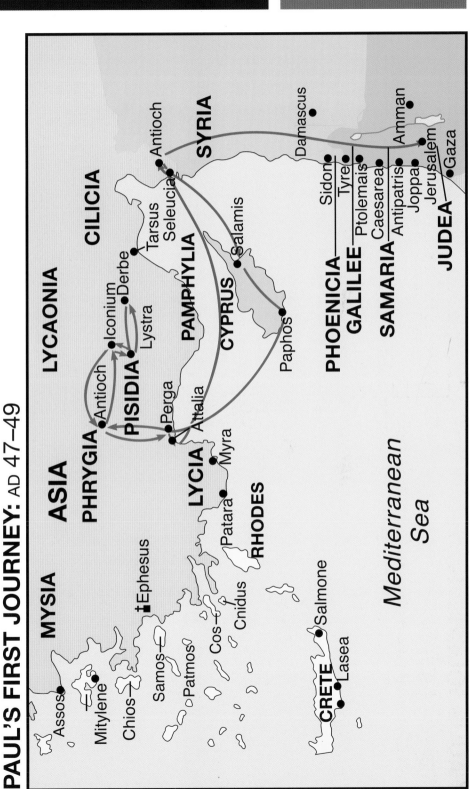

PAUL'S FIRST JOURNEY: AD 47–49

SYRIA

CILICIA

LYCAONIA

CYPRUS

PAMPHYLIA

PISIDIA

PHRYGIA

ASIA

MYSIA

LYCIA

RHODES

PHOENICIA

GALILEE

SAMARIA

JUDEA

Damascus

Amman

Gaza

Sidon

Tyre

Ptolemais

Caesarea

Antipatris

Joppa

Jerusalem

Antioch

Tarsus

Seleucia

Salamis

Paphos

Iconium

Derbe

Lystra

Antioch

Perga

Attalia

Myra

Patara

Cnidus

Cos

Samos

Patmos

Chios

‡Ephesus

Mitylene

Assos

Salmone

Lasea

CRETE

Mediterranean Sea

PAUL'S SECOND JOURNEY: AD 49–51

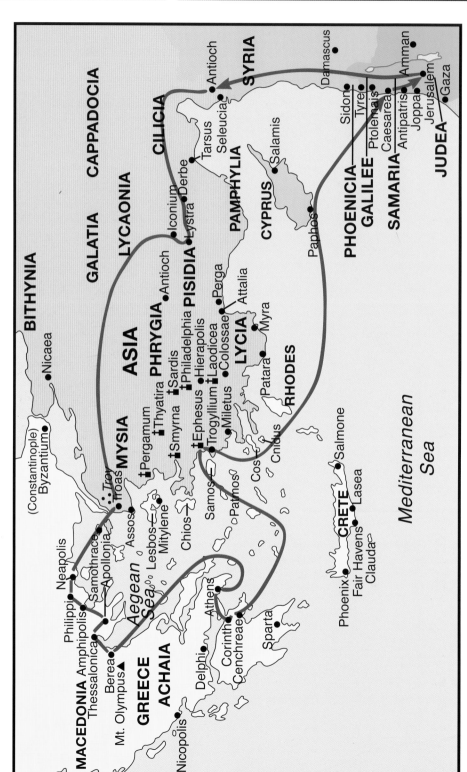

PAUL'S THIRD JOURNEY: AD 52–57

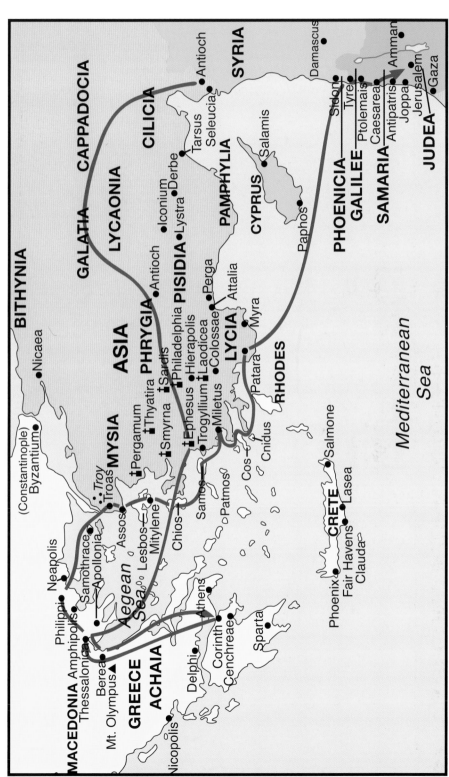

PAUL'S JOURNEY TO ROME: AD 57–62

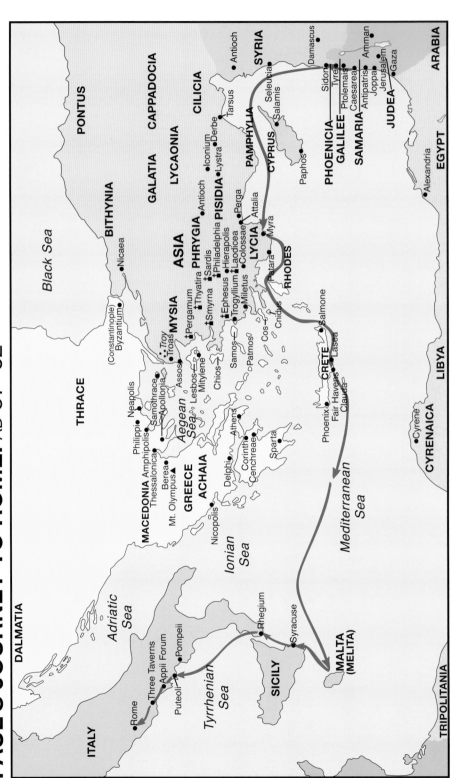

Where to Find
Favorite
Bible Verses

Salvation Verses

Verses of Comfort and Strength

100 Key People and Events

Teachings and Parables of Jesus

GOD

The Only God

Hear, O Israel: The Lord our God, the Lord is one. – *Deuteronomy 6:4*

I am the first and I am the last; apart from me there is no God. – *Isaiah 44:6*

I am the Lord, and there is no other. – *Isaiah 45:5*

Worship the Lord your God, and serve him only – *Matthew 4:10*

Almighty Lord

Great is the Lord, and most worthy of praise. – *Psalm 48:1*

[God] determines the number of the stars and calls each of them by name. – *Psalm 147:4–5*

As the heavens are higher than the earth, so are my ways higher than your ways. – *Isaiah 55:8–9*

For nothing is impossible with God. – *Luke 1:37*

Loving Creator

What is man that you are mindful of him?... You crowned him with glory and honor. – *Psalm 8:4–5*

Know that the Lord is God. ... [We are] the sheep of his pasture. – *Psalm 100:3*

You knit me together in my mother's womb .... I am fearfully and wonderfully made. – *Psalm 139:13–16*

The very hairs of your head are all numbered .... You are worth more than many sparrows. – *Luke 12:6–7*

HOLY SPIRIT

Guides Us

[God] will give you another Counselor to be with you forever. – *John 14:16*

The Holy Spirit ... will teach you all things. – *John 14:26*

[When] the Spirit of truth comes, he will guide you into all truth. – *John 16:13*

Empowers Us

But you will receive power when the Holy Spirit comes on you. – *Acts 1:8*

[The disciples] were filled with the Holy Spirit and began to speak in other tongues. – *Acts 2:4*

There are different kinds of gifts, but the same Spirit. – *1 Corinthians 12:4–13*

I pray that ... [the Father] may strengthen you with power through his Spirit in your inner being. – *Ephesians 3:16*

Lives in Us

The Spirit himself intercedes for us with groans that words cannot express. – *Romans 8:26*

Your body is a temple of the Holy Spirit, who is in you. – *1 Corinthians 6:19*

God sent the Spirit of his Son into our hearts, the Spirit who calls out, "Abba, Father." – *Galatians 4:6*

You were marked in him with a seal, the promised Holy Spirit who is a deposit. – *Ephesians 1:13–14*

NAMES OF GOD

Adoni	The Great Lord	Psalm 8
El / Elohim	The Strong One	Exodus 15:2
El Shaddai	All-Sufficient One	Genesis 17:1–3
Jehovah-Jireh	The Lord Will Provide	Genesis 22:13–14
Jehovah-Rapha	The Lord Who Heals	Exodus 15:25–27
Jehovah-Shalom	The Lord is Peace	Numbers 6:22–27
YHWH	I AM	Exodus 3:14

JESUS

Our Savior

For the Son of Man came to seek and to save what was lost. – *Luke 19:10*

In the beginning was the Word. ... The Word became flesh and made his dwelling among us. – *John 1:1–14*

I have come that they may have life, and have it to the full. – *John 10:10*

I am the resurrection and the life. ... He who believes in me will live.
– *John 11:25–26*

I am the way and the truth and the life. No one comes to the Father except through me. – *John 14:6*

Salvation is found in no one else. – *Acts 4:12*

Loving Lord and Teacher

If you hold to my teaching ... you will know the truth, and the truth will set you free.
– *John 8:31–32*

You call me "Teacher" and "Lord." ... I have set an example [for you]. – *John 13:13–15*

How wide and long and high and deep is the love of Christ. – *Ephesians 3:18*

At the name of Jesus every knee should bow ... and every tongue confess that Jesus Christ is Lord. – *Philippians 2:10–11*

Coming Again in Glory

Men will see the Son of Man coming in clouds with great power and glory.
– *Mark 13:26*

In my Father's house are many rooms. ... I will come back and take you to be with me. – *John 14:2–3*

Jesus ... will come back in the same way you have seen him go into heaven.
– *Acts 1:11*

NAMES OF JESUS	
Alpha and Omega	Revelation 21:6
Bread of Life	John 6:35
Bridegroom	Matthew 9:15; John 3:29
Bright Morning Star	Revelation 22:16
Cornerstone	Ephesians 2:20; 1 Peter 2:6
Good Shepherd	John 10:14
Immanuel	Matthew 1:23
Light of the World	John 8:12
Prince of Peace	Isaiah 9:6
True Vine	John 15:5

TRINITY

There is only one God, and this one God is in three Persons. The Bible teaches that God the Father, the Son, and the Holy Spirit each possess the divine attributes.

THE TRINITY			
Divine Attribute	**Father**	**Son**	**Holy Spirit**
Eternal	Romans 16:26–27	Revelation 1:17	Hebrews 9:14
Creator of All	Psalm 100:3	Colossians 1:16	Psalm 104:30
Omnipresent	Jeremiah 23:24	Ephesians 1:23	Psalm 139:7
All-knowing	1 John 3:20	John 21:17	1 Corinthians 2:10
Acts supernaturally	Ephesians 1:5	Matthew 8:3	1 Corinthians 12:11
Gives Life	Genesis 1:11–31	John 1:4	Romans 8:10–11
Strengthens Believers	Psalm 138:3	Philippians 4:13	Ephesians 3:16

SHARING JESUS

The Bible teaches that believers are called to share the good news (the Gospel) of Jesus with others in a spirit of boldness and kindness.

How beautiful ... are the feet of those who bring good news. *– Isaiah 52:7*

You are the light of the world. ... Let your light shine before men. *– Matthew 5:14–16*

I am not ashamed of the gospel, because it is the power of God. *– Romans 1:16*

Let your conversation be always full of grace, seasoned with salt. *– Colossians 4:5–6*

For God did not give us a spirit of timidity, but a spirit of power. *– 2 Timothy 1:7*

I am not ashamed, because I know whom I have believed. *– 2 Timothy 1:12*

Preach the Word; be prepared in season and out of season. *– 2 Timothy 4:2*

Always be prepared to give an answer to everyone who asks. *– 1 Peter 3:15*

Sin and Its Consequences

The heart is deceitful above all things. *– Jeremiah 17:9*

For all have sinned and fall short of the glory of God. *– Romans 3:23*

Just as sin entered the world through one man ... all sinned. *– Romans 5:12*

For the wages of sin is death, but the gift of God is eternal life. *– Romans 6:23*

Jesus' Sacrifice for Us

[Christ] was despised and rejected.... By his wounds we are healed. *– Isaiah 53:3–5*

For God so loved the world that he gave his one and only Son. *– John 3:16–18*

God presented [Jesus] as a sacrifice of atonement. *– Romans 3:25*

God demonstrates his own love for us in this: while we were still sinners, Christ died for us. *– Romans 5:8*

Christ died for our sins.... He was buried [and] raised on the third day. *– 1 Corinthians 15:3–4*

God was pleased ... to reconcile to himself all things ... by making peace through [Jesus'] blood, shed on the cross. *– Colossians 1:19–20*

Believing in Jesus

I am the resurrection and the life. He who believes in me will live. *– John 11:25*

Everyone who calls on the name of the Lord will be saved. *– Acts 2:21*

If you confess with your mouth, "Jesus is Lord," and believe in your heart that God raised him from the dead, you will be saved. *– Romans 10:9*

By grace you have been saved, through faith ... not by works. *– Ephesians 2:8–9*

If we confess our sins, he is faithful and just and will forgive us our sins. *– 1 John 1:9*

I stand at the door and knock. If anyone hears my voice... *– Revelation 3:20*

Our New Life

Though your sins be like scarlet, they shall be white as snow. *– Isaiah 1:18*

There is now no condemnation for those who are in Christ Jesus. *– Romans 8:1–2*

Having been justified by his grace, we might become heirs having the hope of eternal life. *– Titus 3:4–7*

God has given us eternal life.... He who has the Son has life. *– 1 John 5:11–12*

A New Identity and a New Name

When people decide to believe in Jesus and follow him, they are given new names and blessings, not because they earned it, but because of God's love and mercy.

Believers in Jesus are:

Accepted Romans 15:7	**Alive with Christ** Ephesians 2:4–5	**Baptized into Christ** Romans 6:3–4
Body of Christ 1 Corinthians 12:27	**Born Again** John 3:3-7	**Called** Romans 8:28–30
Children of God 1 John 3:1–2	**Children of Promise** Galatians 4:28	**Chosen** 2 Thessalonians 2:13
Citizens of Heaven Philippians 3:20	**Empowered by God** Ephesians 6:10-17	**Entrusted with the Secrets of God** 1 Corinthians 4:1
Fishers of Men Mark 1:17	**Forgiven** Colossians 2:13	**Friends of Jesus** John 15:15
Holy 1 Peter 1:15–16	**Instruments for Noble Purposes** 2 Timothy 2:20-21	**Lights in the World** Matthew 5:14–16
Loved 1 John 4:10	**Ministers of Reconciliation** 2 Corinthians 5:18	**New Creations** 2 Corinthians 5:17
One in Him Galatians 3:28	**Purified** 1 John 1:9	**Raised with Christ** Colossians 3:1
Redeemed 1 Peter 1:18–19	**Royal Priesthood** 1 Peter 2:9	**Saints** Romans 1:7
Saved Acts 16:30–31	**Servants of God** 2 Corinthians 6:4	**Soldiers of Christ** 2 Timothy 2:3
Special People 1 Peter 2:9	**Temple of the Holy Spirit** 1 Corinthians 6:19	**Victorious** 1 Corinthians 15:57

WORDS OF COMFORT AND STRENGTH

Afraid

I will never leave you nor forsake you.— *Joshua 1:5*

Who knows but that you have come to royal position for such a time as this?— *Esther 4:14*

We trust in the name of the Lord our God.— *Psalm 20:7*

Though I walk through the valley of the shadow of death, I will fear no evil.— *Psalm 23*

The Lord is my light and my salvation—whom shall I fear?— *Psalm 27:1*

In God I trust; I will not be afraid.— *Psalm 56:11*

Do not fret because of evil men.... The lamp of the wicked will be snuffed out.— *Proverbs 24:19–20*

I am the Lord your God who takes hold of your right hand … Do not fear.— *Isaiah 41:13*

Fear not, for I have redeemed you; I have summoned you by name.— *Isaiah 43:1*

The Lord your God is with you, he is mighty to save.— *Zephaniah 3:17*

Do not be afraid of those who kill the body but cannot kill the soul.— *Matthew 10:28*

If God is for us, who can be against us?— *Romans 8:31*

Angry

A gentle answer turns away wrath, but a harsh word stirs up anger.— *Proverbs 15:1*

Do not let the sun go down while you are still angry.— *Ephesians 4:26*

Be quick to listen, slow to speak and slow to become angry.— *James 1:19*

Do not repay evil with evil or insult with insult.— *1 Peter 3:9*

Backsliding

If my people who are called by my name will humble themselves … [I] will forgive their sin and heal their land.— *2 Chronicles 7:14*

Create in me a pure heart, O God.— *Psalm 51:10–12*

The Lord is compassionate … slow to anger, abounding in love.— *Psalm 103:8*

The Lord disciplines those he loves.— *Hebrews 12:5–11*

Come near to God and he will come near to you.— *James 4:8*

If we confess our sins, he is faithful and just and will forgive us our sins.— *1 John 1:9*

Confused

Though he stumble, he will not fall, for the Lord upholds him.— *Psalm 37:23–24*

Trust in the Lord with all your heart and lean not on your own understanding.— *Prov. 3:5–6*

I am doing a new thing!... Do you not perceive it? I am making a way in the desert and streams in the wasteland.— *Isaiah 43:19*

For I know the plans I have for you … plans to prosper you.— *Jeremiah 29:11*

In all things God works for the good of those who love him.— *Romans 8:28*

If any of you lack wisdom, he should ask God.— *James 1:5*

Depressed

The Lord bless you and keep you; The Lord make his face shine upon you.— *Num. 6:24–26*

Do not grieve, for the joy of the Lord is your strength.— *Nehemiah 8:10*

As the deer pants for streams of water, so my soul pants for you.— *Psalm 42:1–2*

[The Lord] heals the brokenhearted and binds up their wounds.— *Psalm 147:3*

He has sent me to bind up the brokenhearted.— *Isaiah 61:1*

His compassions never fail. They are new every morning.— *Lamentations 3:22–23*

In this world you will have trouble.... Take heart! I have overcome the world.— *John 16:33*

Whatever is true, whatever is noble … think about such things.— *Philippians 4:8–9*

WHEN YOU ARE...

Doubting Salvation

As far as the east is from the west, so far has he removed our [sins] from us. – *Psalm 103:12*

Whoever hears my word and believes ... has crossed over from death to life. – *John 5:24*

I tell you the truth, he who believes has everlasting life. – *John 6:47*

I give them eternal life.... No one can snatch them out of my hand. – *John 10:28*

He who began a good work in you will carry it on to completion. – *Philippians 1:6*

Envious

Delight yourself in the Lord and he will give you the desires of your heart. – *Psalm 37:4*

Give me neither property nor riches, but give me only my daily bread. – *Proverbs 30:8–9*

I have learned to be content whatever the circumstances. – *Philippians 4:11*

Keep your lives free from the love of money and be content with what you have. – *Hebrews 13:5*

Grieving

[God] will swallow up death forever.... [He] will wipe away the tears. – *Isaiah 25:8*

Blessed are those who mourn, for they will be comforted. – *Matthew 5:4*

Death has been swallowed up.... Where, O death, is your victory? – *1 Corinthians 15:54-57*

As long as we are at home in the body we are away from the Lord. – *2 Corinthians 5:6*

We do not want you to ... grieve like [those] who have no hope. – *1 Thessalonians 4:13–18*

Harmed

You intended to harm me, but God intended it for good. – *Genesis 50:20*

If your enemy is hungry, give him food to eat. – *Proverbs 25:21*

Blessed are those who are persecuted because of righteousness. – *Matthew 5:10–12*

[If] your brother has something against you ... first go and be reconciled. – *Matthew 5:23–24*

If you forgive men ... your heavenly Father will also forgive you. – *Matthew 6:14*

If he sins against you seven times in a day ... forgive him. – *Luke 17:3–4*

Ill (physical suffering)

The Lord is my shepherd, I shall not be in want. – *Psalm 23*

Though outwardly we are wasting away, yet inwardly we are being renewed ....
   We fix our eyes not on what is seen, but on what is unseen. – *2 Corinthians 4:16–18*

The prayer offered in faith will make the sick person well. – *James 5:14–15*

Impatient

[God] has made everything beautiful in its time. – *Ecclesiastes 3:1–11*

Wait for the Lord; be strong and take heart. – *Psalm 27:14*

I waited patiently for the Lord .... He set my feet on a rock. – *Psalm 40:1–2*

Be completely ... patient, bearing with one another in love. – *Ephesians 4:2*

Clothe yourselves with compassion, kindness ... and patience. – *Colossians 3:12*

The Lord's servant must not quarrel.... [He] must be kind to everyone. – *2 Timothy 2:22–23*

Lonely

[The Lord] satisfies the thirsty and fills the hungry with good things. – *Psalm 107:9*

O Lord, you have searched me and you know me. – *Psalm 139:1–10*

I am with you always, to the very end of the age. – *Matthew 28:20*

You will leave me all alone. Yet I am not alone, for my Father is with me. – *John 16:32*

Neither height nor depth ... will be able to separate us from the love of God. – *Romans 8:39*

WHEN YOU ARE...

Suffering

I know that my Redeemer lives …. He will stand upon the earth. – *Job 19:25–27*

The Lord is my rock, my fortress and my deliverer. – *Psalm 18:2*

This poor man called, and … [the Lord] saved him out of all his troubles. – *Psalm 34:6*

I lift up my eyes to the hills—where does my help come from? My help comes from the Lord.
– *Psalm 121:1–2*

The Lord longs to be gracious …. How gracious he will be when you cry for help!
– *Isaiah 30:18–19*

I will strengthen you …. I will uphold you with my righteous right hand. – *Isaiah 41:10*

We are hard pressed … but not crushed…. Persecuted, but not abandoned.
– *2 Corinthians 4:7–9*

These [sufferings] have come so that your faith … refined by fire—may be proved genuine.
– *1 Peter 1:6–7*

Tempted

And lead us not into temptation, but deliver us from the evil one. – *Matthew 6:13*

The spirit is willing but the body is weak. – *Matthew 26:41*

Pray that you will not fall into temptation. – *Luke 22:40*

He will not let you be tempted beyond what you can bear. – *1 Corinthians 10:13*

Because [Jesus] … was tempted, he is able to help those who are being tempted.
– *Hebrews 2:18*

When tempted no one should say, "God is tempting me." – *James 1:13–15*

Resist the devil, and he will flee from you. – *James 4:7*

Tired

The Lord, is my strength and my song. – *Isaiah 12:2*

Those who hope in the Lord will renew their strength. They will soar on wings like eagles.
– *Isaiah 40:28–31*

Come to me, all you who are weary …. My yoke is easy and my burden is light.
– *Matthew 11:28–30*

My grace is sufficient for you, for my power is made perfect in weakness. – *2 Corinthians 12:9*

I can do everything through him who gives me strength. – *Philippians 4:13*

I have fought the good fight … I have kept the faith. – *2 Timothy 4:7*

[God] will not forget your work …. [Show] diligence to the very end. – *Hebrews 6:10–12*

Let us run [the race] with perseverance…. Let us fix our eyes on Jesus. – *Hebrews 12:1–3*

The testing of your faith develops perseverance. – *James 1:2–4*

Worried

Trust in the Lord with all your heart and lean not on your own understanding. – *Proverbs 3:5–6*

[He] who trusts in the Lord … will be like a tree planted by the water. – *Jeremiah 17:7–8*

"Not by might, nor by power, but by my Spirit" says the Lord. – *Zechariah 4:6*

Do not worry about tomorrow, for tomorrow will take care of itself. – *Matthew 6:34*

Do not be anxious about anything, but in everything, by prayer … – *Philippians 4:6–7*

And my God will meet all your needs according to his glorious riches. – *Philippians 4:19*

Cast all your anxiety on him because he cares for you. – *1 Peter 5:7*

OLD TESTAMENT EVENTS

Creation of the World – *Genesis 1*
The Fall (Adam and Eve) – *Genesis 3*
Noah's Ark and the Flood – *Genesis 6–8*
Tower of Babel – *Genesis 11:1–9*
Call of Abraham – *Genesis 12:1–3*
Abrahamic Covenant – *Genesis 15*
Hagar and Ishmael – *Genesis 16; 21:8–21*
Sodom and Gomorrah (Lot) – *Genesis 19*
Birth of Isaac – *Genesis 21:1–7*
Abraham's Offering of Isaac – *Genesis 22:1–18*
Esau and Jacob – *Genesis 25:21–34; 27:1–28:9*
Jacob, Leah and Rachel – *Genesis 29:1–30:24*
Joseph and his Brothers – *Genesis 37, 39–47*
Finding of Baby Moses – *Exodus 2:1–10*
Moses and the Burning Bush – *Exodus 3:1–10*
Ten Plagues and Passover – *Exodus 7:14–12:30*
Parting of the Red Sea – *Exodus 14:16–31*
Water from a Rock – *Exodus 17:1–7 (Numbers 20)*
Ten Commandments – *Exodus 20:3–17*
The Tabernacle – *Exodus 25–30*
Worship of the Golden Calf – *Exodus 32:1–6*
Spies Sent into Canaan – *Numbers 13*
The Bronze Snake – *Numbers 21:4–9*
Rahab Hides the Spies – *Joshua 2*
Fall of Jericho – *Joshua 6:1–25*
Deborah (Barak and Jael) – *Judges 4*
Gideon – *Judges 6–8*
Samson and Delilah – *Judges 13–16*
Hannah and Samuel – *1 Samuel 1–3*
Saul Anointed King – *1 Samuel 8–10*
David Anointed King – *1 Samuel 16:1–13*
David and Goliath – *1 Samuel 17:4–51*
David and Jonathan – *1 Samuel 20*
Saul and the Witch of Endor – *1 Samuel 28*
David and Bathsheba – *2 Samuel 11:1–12:25*
Solomon Asks for Wisdom – *1 Kings 3:5–15*
Solomon Judges Between Two Women – *1 Kings 3:16–28*
The First Temple – *1 Kings 6, 8:1–9*
Queen of Sheba Visits Solomon – *1 Kings 10:1–13*
United Kingdom Divides – *1 Kings 12:1–20*
Elijah and the Prophets of Baal – *1 Kings 18:20–40*
Elijah and the Chariot of Fire – *2 Kings 2:1–11*
Elisha and the Shunammite – *2 Kings 4:8–37*
Hezekiah's Illness – *2 Kings 20:1–11*
Josiah Renews the Covenant – *2 Kings 23:1–25*
Fall of Jerusalem – *2 Chronicles 36:14–21*
Daniel Interprets Dreams – *Daniel 2:24–45*
The Furnace of Fire – *Daniel 3*
Daniel in the Lion's Den – *Daniel 6*
The Second Temple – *2 Chronicles 36:22–23; Ezra 3:10–13*

TEACHINGS & PARABLES OF JESUS

Beatitudes/Sermon on the Mount – *Matthew 5:1–7:29*
Golden Rule – *Matthew 7:12; Luke 6:31*
Good Samaritan – *Luke 10:25–37*
Great Commission – *Matthew 28:18–20; Mark 16:15–16*
Greatest Commandment – *Matthew 22:34–40; Mark 12:28–34*
Hidden Treasure/Valuable Pearl – *Matthew 13:44–46*
Lord's Prayer – *Matthew 6:9–13; Luke 11:1–4*
Lost Sheep – *Matthew 18:10–14; Luke 15:1–7*
Mustard Seed – *Matthew 13:31–32; Mark 4:30–32; Luke 13:18–19*
Pearl of Great Price – *Matthew 13:45–46*
Persistent Widow – *Luke 18:2–8*
Prodigal Son – *Luke 15:11–32*
Rich Man and Lazarus – *Luke 16:19–31*
Sheep and Goats – *Matthew 25:31–46*
Shrewd Manager – *Luke 16:1–13*
Sower and the Seeds – *Matthew 13:1–23; Mark 4:1–20; Luke 8:4–15*
Talents – *Matthew 25:14–30; Luke 19:12–27*
Ten Virgins – *Matthew 25:1–13*
Unmerciful Servant – *Matthew 18:21–35*

BOOK OF ACTS – THE EARLY CHURCH

Ascension – *1:1–11*
Pentecost – *2:1–13*
Peter Before the Sanhedrin – *4:5–22*
Ananias and Sapphira – *5:1–11*
Stephen's Martyrdom – *6:8–7:60*
The Ethiopian Eunuch – *8:26–40*
Saul's Conversion – *9:1–19*
Raising of Dorcas – *9:36–42*
Conversion of Cornelius – *10:23–48*
Peter Rescued from Prison – *12:1–19*
Herod Agrippa Struck Dead – *12:20–23*
Paul's First Missionary Journey – *13:1–5*
Paul's Second Missionary Journey – *15:36–16:5*
Conversion of Lydia – *16:13–15*
Conversion of a Jailer – *16:25–34*
Paul's Mars Hill Address – *17:16–34*
Paul's Third Missionary Journey – *18:22–23*
Raising of Eutychus – *20:7–12*
Paul Seized in the Temple – *21:27–36*
Paul Rescued by Roman Soldiers – *22:22–30*
Paul Escapes a Plot to Kill Him – *23:12–24*
Paul Appeals to Caesar – *25:11–12*
Paul Before Festus and Agrippa – *25:23–26:32*

THE LIFE OF JESUS

Life of Jesus	Matthew	Mark	Luke	John
Birth in Bethlehem	1:18–25		2:1–20	
Childhood	2:1–23		2:21–52	
Baptized	3:13–17	1:9–11	3:21–22	1:29–34
Tempted in the Wilderness	4:1–11	1:12–13	4:1–13	
Changes Water into Wine				2:1–11
Speaks with Nicodemus				3:1–21
Speaks with the Samaritan Woman				4:4–26
Heals a Man with Leprosy	8:1–4	1:40–45	5:12–14	
Heals a Paralyzed Man	9:1–8	2:1–12	5:17–26	
Heals the Centurion's Servant	8:5-13		7:1–10	
Raises a Widow's Son from the Dead			7:11–17	
Anointed by a Forgiven Woman			7:36–50	
Calms the Storm	8:23–27	4:35–41	8:22–25	
Casts out Demons	8:28–34	5:1–20	8:26–39	
Heals the Woman who Touched his Cloak	9:20–22	5:25–34	8:43–48	
Feeds the crowd of 5,000	14:13–21	6:32–44	9:10–17	6:1–13
Walks on Water	14:22–33	6:45–51		6:16–21
Peter's Confession of Christ	16:13–20	8:27–30	9:18–22	
Transfiguration	17:1–8	9:2–8	9:28–36	
Forgives the Woman Caught in Adultery				8:2–11
Visits with Mary and Martha			10:38–42	
Heals a Man Born Blind				9:1–7
Raises Lazarus from the Dead				11:1–44
Heals Ten People with Leprosy			17:11–19	
Speaks with the Rich Young Man	19:16–30	10:17–31	18:18–30	
Zacchaeus the Tax Collector			19:1–10	
Palm Sunday	21:1–11	11:1–10	19:28–38	12:12–15
Clears the Temple	21:12–13	11:15–17	19:45–46	
The Last Supper	26:17–30	14:12–26	22:7–38	13:1–30
In the Garden of Gethsemane	26:36–56	14:32–50	22:39–53	18:1–11
Suffers and Dies on the Cross	27:26–50	15:16–37	22:63–23:46	19:1–30
Resurrection and Ascension	28:1–20	16:1–19	24:1–53	20:1–18

TOPICS (KEY PHRASES SHOWN)

ANGELS

For he will command his angels concerning you to guard you. – *Psalm 91:11*

For I tell you that [these children's] angels in heaven always see. – *Matthew 18:10*

ARMOR OF GOD

Put on the full armor of God. – *Ephesians 6:13–18*

BAPTISM

I baptize you with water, but he will baptize you with the Holy Spirit. – *Mark 1:8*

We were therefore buried with him through baptism. – *Romans 6:4*

BIBLE (WORD)

I have hidden your word in my heart. – *Psalm 119:11*

Your word is a lamp to my feet and a light to my path. – *Psalm 119:105*

My word ... will not return to me empty.

– *Isaiah 55:11*

All Scripture is God-breathed and is useful ... – *2 Timothy 3:16*

The word of God is ... sharper than any double-edged sword. – *Hebrews 4:12*

CHILDLESSNESS

More are the children of the desolate woman.... – *Isaiah 54:1–3*

CHILDREN

Unless you ... become like little children, you will never enter the kingdom. – *Matthew 18:3*

But if anyone causes one of these little ones who believe in me to sin... – *Matthew 18:6*

Let the little children come to me. – *Matthew 19:14*

Children, obey your parents in the Lord. – *Ephesians 6:1*

CHURCH

On this rock I will build my church. – *Matthew16:18*

Let us not give up meeting together. – *Hebrews 10:25*

COMMITMENT TO GOD

[Choose] this day whom you will serve.... As for me and my household, we will serve the Lord. – *Joshua 24:15*

Your people will be my people and your God my God. – *Ruth 1:16*

Seek first his kingdom and his righteousness. – *Matthew 6:33*

Whoever disowns me before men, I will disown him. – *Matthew 10:32–33*

He must deny himself and take up his cross daily and follow me. – *Luke 9:23*

Whoever loses his life for me and for the gospel will save it. – *Mark 8:35*

I have been crucified with Christ and I no longer live. – *Galatians 2:20*

For to me, to live is Christ and to die is gain. – *Philippians 1:21*

DIVORCE

"I hate divorce" says the Lord. – *Malachi 2:16*

Anyone who divorces ... except for marital unfaithfulness .... – *Matthew 5:32*

If the unbeliever leaves, let him do so.... – *1 Corinthians 7:15*

DRUNKENNESS

Drunkards and gluttons become poor. – *Proverbs 23:21*

Do not get drunk on wine .... Instead, be filled with the Spirit. – *Ephesians 5:18*

END TIMES

You will hear of wars and rumors of wars. – *Matthew 24:6*

Keep watch because you do not know on what day your Lord will come. – *Matthew 24:42*

[We] will be caught up together with them in the clouds. – *1 Thessalonians 4:17*

The Lord will come like a thief in the night. – *1 Thessalonians 5:2*

With the Lord a day is like a thousand years. – *2 Peter 3:8-10*

FAITH

If you have faith as small as a mustard seed, you can [move mountains.] – *Matthew 17:20*

Faith comes from hearing the message ... through the word of Christ. – *Romans 10:17*

Now faith is being sure of what we hope for. – *Hebrews 11:1*

Without faith it is impossible to please God. – *Hebrews 11:6*

TOPICS (KEY PHRASES SHOWN)

FALSE TEACHERS

False prophets … come to you in sheep's clothing. – *Matthew 7:15*

[If] an angel from heaven should preach [another] gospel … let him be eternally condemned! – *Galatians 1:8*

FRIENDSHIP

A friend loves at all times. – *Proverbs 17:17*

As iron sharpens iron, so one man sharpens another. – *Proverbs 27:17*

A cord of three strands is not quickly broken. – *Ecclesiastes 4:12*

FRUIT OF THE SPIRIT

The fruit of the Spirit is love, joy, peace … – *Galatians 5:22–23*

GIVING

A generous man will prosper. – *Proverbs 11:24–25*

Bring the whole tithe … [and I will] pour out so much blessing. – *Malachi 3:10*

God loves a cheerful giver. – *2 Corinthians 9:7*

GOOD WORKS

Whatever you did for one of the least of these … you did for me. – *Matthew 25:40*

If your enemy is hungry, feed him …. Overcome evil with good. – *Romans 12:20-21*

A man reaps what he sows…. Let us not become weary in doing good. – *Galatians 6:7–11*

We are God's workmanship, created … to do good works. – *Ephesians 2:10*

Look not only to your own interests, but also to the interests of others. – *Philippians 2:4*

Do not merely listen to the word …. Do what it says. – *James 1:22*

[Pure] religion … is this: to look after orphans and widows. – *James 1:27*

Faith by itself if it is not accompanied by action, is dead. – *James 2:17*

GOSSIPING

To see many good days, keep your tongue from evil. – *Psalm 34:12–13*

A gossip betrays a confidence. – *Proverbs 11:13*

Whoever repeats the matter separates close friends. – *Proverbs 17:9*

[Speak] only what is helpful for building others up. – *Ephesians 4:29*

GOVERNMENT

Then give to Caesar what is Caesar's, and to God what is God's. – *Luke 20:25*

We must obey God rather than men! – *Acts 5:28–29*

Be subject to rulers and authorities. – *Titus 3:1*

HEAVEN

The wolf will live with the lamb … and the lion [with] the yearling. – *Isaiah 11:6*

They will enter Zion with singing … sorrow and sighing will flee away. – *Isaiah 51:11*

In my Father's house are many rooms…. I am going there to prepare a place for you. – *John 14:1–3*

Now we see but a poor reflection as in a mirror. [When perfection comes] we shall see face to face. – *1 Corinthians 13:10–13*

Our citizenship is in heaven. – *Philippians 3:20*

When he appears, we shall be like him, for we shall see him as he is. – *1 John 3:2*

[God] will wipe every tear from their eyes. – *Revelation 21:4*

They will see [God's] face, and his name will be on their foreheads. – *Revelation 22:4*

HELL

Better for you to enter life crippled than to have two feet and be thrown into hell. – *Mark 9:45–47*

If anyone's name was not in the book of life, he was thrown into the lake of fire. – *Revelation 20:14–15*

HUMILITY & PRIDE

Pride goes before destruction, a haughty spirit before a fall. – *Proverbs 16:18*

In humility consider others better than yourselves. – *Philippians 2:3*

Humble yourselves before the Lord, and he will lift you up. – *James 4:10*

God opposes the proud but gives grace to the humble. – *1 Peter 5:5-6*

HYPOCRISY

Man looks at the outward appearance, but the Lord looks at the heart. – *1 Samuel 16:7*

[They] honor me with their lips, but their hearts are far from me. – *Isaiah 29:13*

Do not judge…. First take the plank out of your own eye. – *Matthew 7:1–5*

You hypocrites! You are like whitewashed tombs. – *Matthew 23:27*

TOPICS (KEY PHRASES SHOWN)

JUSTICE

Do not pervert justice; do not show partiality.
– *Leviticus 19:15*

Defend the cause of the weak…. Maintain the rights of the poor. – *Psalm 82:3–4*

For the Lord is a God of justice. – *Isaiah 30:18*

What does the Lord require of you? To act justly and to love mercy. – *Micah 6:8*

I will come near to you for judgment … [against] those who defraud. – *Malachi 3:5*

KINDNESS & MERCY

For I desire mercy, not sacrifice. – *Hosea 6:6*

Do to others as you would have them do to you. – *Luke 6:31*

Clothe yourselves with compassion, kindness … gentleness and patience. – *Colossians 3:12*

LAW

Do not think that I have come to abolish the Law or the Prophets. – *Matthew 5:17–18*

Now that faith has come, we are no longer under … the law. – *Galatians 3:25*

LORD'S SUPPER

This is my body given for you; do this in remembrance of me. – *Luke 22:19*

Whenever you eat this bread … you proclaim the Lord's death. – *1 Corinthians 11:26*

LOVE

Love the Lord your God with all of your heart. – *Matthew 22:37*

[All] will know that you are my disciples, if you love one another. – *John 13:34–35*

Greater love has no one that this, that he lay down his life for his friends. – *John 15:13*

Love is patient, love is kind – *1 Corinthians 13*

Let us not love with words or tongue, but with actions. – *1 John 3:18*

Love covers over a multitude of sins. – *1 Peter 4:8*

Let us love one another, for love comes from God. – *1 John 4:7*

MARRIAGE

A man will leave his father and mother and be united to his wife. – *Genesis 2:24*

Rejoice in the wife of your youth. – *Prov. 5:18-20*

Do not be yoked together with unbelievers. – *2 Corinthians 6:14*

Wives, submit to your husbands …. Husbands, love your wives. – *Ephesians 5:21-33*

Marriage should be honored by all, and the marriage bed kept pure. – *Hebrews 13:4*

Husbands … be considerate as you live with your wives. – *1 Peter 3:7*

MISSIONS

Whom shall I send?... Here am I. Send me! – *Isaiah 6:8*

Therefore go and make disciples of all nations. – *Matthew 28:18–20*

You will be my witnesses … to the ends of the earth. – *Acts 1:8*

How can they believe in the one of whom they have not heard? – *Romans 10:14*

I have become all things to all men … [to] save some. – *1 Corinthians 9:20–22*

MONEY (WEALTH)

Remember … it is [the Lord] who gives you the ability to produce wealth. – *Deuteronomy 8:18*

The Lord gave and the Lord has taken away. – *Job 1:21*

Honor the Lord with your wealth. – *Proverbs 3:9*

Do not store up for yourselves treasures on earth. – *Matthew 6:19–21*

You cannot serve both God and Money. – *Matthew 6:24*

It is easier for a camel to go through the eye of a needle than for a rich man to enter the kingdom of God. – *Matthew 19:24*

So the last will be first, and the first will be last. – *Matthew 20:16*

What good is it for a man to gain the whole world, yet forfeit his soul? – *Mark 8:36*

Everyone who has been given much, much will be demanded. – *Luke 12:48*

Whoever can be trusted with very little can also be trusted with much. – *Luke 16:10*

For the love of money is a root of all kinds of evil. – *1 Timothy 6:10*

OBEDIENCE

Those who honor me I will honor. – *1 Samuel 2:30*

To obey is better than sacrifice. – *1 Samuel 15:22*

If anyone loves me, he will obey my teaching. – *John 14:23*

PARENTING

Impress [God's commandments] on your children. – *Deuteronomy 6:6–9*

Sons are a heritage from the Lord, children a reward from him. – *Psalm 127:3*

TOPICS (KEY PHRASES SHOWN)

Train a child in the way he should go.... – *Prov. 22:6*

Do not exasperate your children; instead bring them up in ... the Lord. – *Ephesians 6:4*

PRAISE & WORSHIP

Enter his gates with thanksgiving and his courts with praise. – *Psalm 100:4*

[Offering] your bodies as living sacrifices ... your spiritual act of worship. – *Romans 12:1*

Whether you eat or drink ... do it all for the glory of God. – *1 Corinthians 10:31*

Rejoice in the Lord always. I will say it again: Rejoice! – *Philippians 4:4*

PRAYER

Seek the Lord while he may be found; call on him while he is near. – *Isaiah 55:6*

Before they call I will answer. – *Isaiah 65:24*

Call to me and I will answer you and tell you great and unsearchable things. – *Jeremiah 33:3*

Ask and it will be given to you; seek and you will find. – *Matthew 7:7-11*

Where two or three come together in my name, there am I. – *Matthew 18:20*

Pray in the Spirit ... with all kinds of prayers and requests. – *Ephesians 6:18*

Pray continually. – *1 Thessalonians 5:17*

The prayer of a righteous man is powerful and effective. – *James 5:16*

If we ask anything according to [God's] will, he hears us. – *1 John 5:14*

SATAN (DEVIL)

Satan himself masquerades as an angel of light. – *2 Corinthians 11:14*

Resist the devil, and he will flee from you. – *James 4:7*

The devil prowls around like a roaring lion looking ... to devour. – *1 Peter 5:8-9*

SEXUAL IMMORALITY

The body is not meant for sexual immorality. – *1 Corinthians 6:13-18*

It is God's will that you should ... avoid sexual immorality. – *1 Thessalonians 4:3*

Neither the sexually immoral ... nor adulterers nor homosexual offenders ... will inherit the kingdom of God. – *1 Corinthians 6:9-10*

SINGLENESS

An unmarried man is concerned about the Lord's affairs. – *1 Corinthians 7:32*

SPIRITUAL GIFTS

We have different gifts, according to the grace given us. – *Romans 12:3-8*

There are different kinds of gifts, but the same Spirit. – *1 Corinthians 12:4-11*

Each one should use whatever gift he has received to serve others. – *1 Peter 4:10*

TRUTHFULNESS

The Lord detests lying lips, but he delights in men who are truthful. – *Proverbs 12:22*

Let your "Yes" be "Yes," and your "No," "No." – *Matthew 5:37*

Put off falsehood and speak truthfully. – *Ephesians 4:25*

UNITY

How good and pleasant it is when brothers live together in unity! – *Psalm 133:1*

I pray ... that all of them may be one. – *John 17:20-21*

For there is neither Jew nor Greek ... for you are all one in Christ. – *Galatians 3:28*

We are all members of one body. – *Ephesians 4:25*

WISDOM

The foolishness of God is wiser than man's wisdom. – *1 Corinthians 1:18-25*

See to it that no one takes you captive through hollow ... philosophy. – *Colossians 2:8*

If any of you lacks wisdom, he should ask God. – *James 1:5*

WORK

Well done, good and faithful servant! – *Matthew 25:21*

[He] must work ... that he may have something to share with those in need. – *Ephesians 4:28*

Work ... as working for the Lord, not for men. – *Colossians 3:23-24*

WORLD

If the world hates you, keep in mind that it hated me first. – *John 15:18*

They are not of the world, even as I am not of it. – *John 17:15-16*

Do not conform any longer to the pattern of this world. – *Romans 12:2*

The weapons we fight with are not weapons of the world. – *2 Corinthians 10:3-5*

Do not love the world or anything in the world. – *1 John 2:15*

Bible Promises

for Hope and Courage

ABUNDANCE OF PEACE

100 Best-Loved Bible Verses

God's Promises for Times of
Sorrow, Fear, and Despair

God's Promises

In His Word, God gave us promises that we can rely on when we need hope and comfort. These promises reveal to us the deepest nature of God and tell us who God is in relation to His people.

When we have problems or when we are afraid, we often begin to imagine the worst-case scenario. We forget that our loving Father holds us in His hands. When fear and doubt about God's faithfulness seem overwhelming, here's a way to refocus:

1. Choose to trust that God is bigger, smarter and more loving than you can imagine. God loves us, and He always keeps His promises. Read and reread God's promises to you. Fill your mind with them.

Trust in the LORD with all your heart and lean not on
your own understanding; in all your ways acknowledge him, and he will make
your paths straight.   —PROVERBS 3:5, 6

2. Resist the temptation to worship the problem—it's a common form of idolatry! It's easy to get so focused on a problem so that we talk about it endlessly instead of praying about it and focusing on God's ability to handle it.

Cast all your anxiety on him because he cares for you.   —I PETER 5:7

3. Regain your joy and peace: Focus on God—on who He is and what He has done for you—and worship Him. Keep His ability, not the problem's overwhelming nature, in the forefront of your mind.

I lift up my eyes to the hills—
where does my help come from?
My help comes from the LORD,
the Maker of heaven and earth.
He will not let your foot slip—
he who watches over you will not slumber.
               —PSALM 121:1-3

4. Pray, thank God, and let Him take care of it!
Do not be anxious about anything, but in everything,
by prayer and petition, with thanksgiving, present your
requests to God. And the peace of God, which transcends
all understanding, will guard your hearts and your minds
in Christ Jesus.   —PHILIPPIANS 4:6, 7

Loneliness

The LORD your God is with you, he is mighty to save. He will take great delight in you, he will quiet you with his love, he will rejoice over you with singing.
—ZEPHANIAH 3:17

The LORD is close to the brokenhearted and saves those who are crushed in spirit.
—PSALM 34:18

Jesus said, "And surely I am with you always, to the very end of the age."
—MATTHEW 28:20

Yet I am always with you; you hold me by my right hand.
—PSALM 73:23

For the LORD will not reject his people; he will never forsake his inheritance. Judgment will again be founded on righteousness, and all the upright in heart will follow it.

—PSALM 94:14, 15

Fear

The LORD is with me; I will not be afraid. What can man do to me? The LORD is with me; he is my helper. I will look in triumph on my enemies.
—PSALM 118:6, 7

Even though I walk through the valley of the shadow of death, I will fear no evil, for you are with me; your rod and your staff, they comfort me.
—PSALM 23:4

The LORD himself goes before you and will be with you; he will never leave you nor forsake you. Do not be afraid; do not be discouraged.
—DEUTERONOMY 31:8

Jesus said, "Peace I leave with you; my peace I give you. I do not give to you as the world gives. Do not let your hearts be troubled and do not be afraid."

—JOHN 14:27

Worry

Do not be anxious about anything, but in everything, by prayer and petition, with thanksgiving, present your requests to God. And the peace of God, which transcends all understanding, will guard your hearts and your minds in Christ Jesus.
—PHILIPPIANS 4:6, 7

Cast all your anxiety on him because he cares for you. —1 PETER 5:7

So do not worry, saying, "What shall we eat?" or "What shall we drink?" or "What shall we wear?" For the pagans run after all these things, and your heavenly Father knows that you need them. But seek first his kingdom and his righteousness, and all these things will be given to you as well. Therefore do not worry about tomorrow, for tomorrow will worry about itself. Each day has enough trouble of its own.
—MATTHEW 6:31-34

Contentment

Wait for the LORD; be strong and take heart and wait for the LORD.
—PSALM 27:14

God is not unjust; he will not forget your work and the love you have shown him as you have helped his people and continue to help them. We want each of you to show this same diligence to the very end, in order to make your hope sure. We do not want you to become lazy, but to imitate those who through faith and patience inherit what has been promised.
—HEBREWS 6:10-12

Naked I came from my mother's womb, and naked I will depart. The LORD gave and the LORD has taken away; may the name of the LORD be praised.
—JOB 1:21

I know what it is to be in need, and I know what it is to have plenty. I have learned the secret of being content in any and every situation, whether well fed or hungry, whether living in plenty or in want. I can do everything through him who gives me strength.
—PHILIPPIANS 4:12, 13

Security

For you created my inmost being; you knit me together in my mother's womb. I praise you because I am fearfully and wonderfully made; your works are wonderful, I know that full well. My frame was not hidden from you when I was made in the secret place. When I was woven together in the depths of the earth, your eyes saw my unformed body. All the days ordained for me were written in your book before one of them came to be.
—PSALM 139:13-16

But those who hope in the LORD will renew their strength. They will soar on wings like eagles; they will run and not grow weary, they will walk and not be faint.
—ISAIAH 40:31

For God did not give us a spirit of timidity, but a spirit of power, of love and of self-discipline.
—2 TIMOTHY 1:7

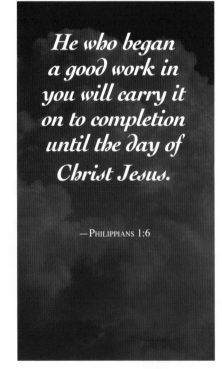

He who began a good work in you will carry it on to completion until the day of Christ Jesus.

—PHILIPPIANS 1:6

Strength and Courage

The LORD is my light and my salvation—whom shall I fear? The LORD is the stronghold of my life—of whom shall I be afraid?

—PSALM 27:1

Be strong and courageous. Do not be afraid or terrified because of them, for the LORD your God goes with you; he will never leave you nor forsake you.

—DEUTERONOMY 31:6

So do not fear, for I am with you; do not be dismayed, for I am your God. I will strengthen you and help you; I will uphold you with my righteous right hand.

—ISAIAH 41:10

Be strong and very courageous. Be careful to obey all the law my servant Moses gave you; do not turn from it to the right or to the left, that you may be successful wherever you go. Do not let this Book of the Law depart from your mouth; meditate on it day and night, so that you may be careful to do everything written in it. Then you will be prosperous and successful.

—JOSHUA 1:7, 8

Comfort

He heals the brokenhearted and binds up their wounds.   —PSALM 147:3

For the Lamb at the center of the throne will be their shepherd; he will lead them to springs of living water. And God will wipe away every tear from their eyes.

—REVELATION 7:17

Even though I walk through the valley of the shadow of death, I will fear no evil, for you are with me; your rod and your staff, they comfort me.

—PSALM 23:4

Jesus said, "Blessed are those who mourn, for they will be comforted."

—MATTHEW 5:4

Peace and Joy

Jesus said, "Peace I leave with you; my peace I give you. I do not give to you as the world gives. Do not let your hearts be troubled and do not be afraid."

—JOHN 14:27

Jesus said, "Come to me, all you who are weary and burdened, and I will give you rest."

—MATTHEW 11:28

Though you have not seen him, you love him; and even though you do not see him now, you believe in him and are filled with an inexpressible and glorious joy, for you are receiving the goal of your faith, the salvation of your souls.

—1 PETER 1:8, 9

Until now you have not asked for anything in my name. Ask and you will receive, and your joy will be complete.

—JOHN 16:24

Now may the Lord of peace himself give you peace at all times and in every way.

—2 THESSALONIANS 3:16

Assurance of Salvation

And this is the testimony: God has given us eternal life, and this life is in his Son. He who has
the Son has life; he who does not have the Son of God does not have life. I write these things
to you who believe in the name of the Son of God so that you may know that you
have eternal life.

—1 JOHN 5:11-13

If you confess with your mouth, "Jesus is Lord,"
and believe in your heart that God raised him from
the dead, you will be saved.

—ROMANS 10:9

For God so loved the world that he gave his one
and only Son, that whoever believes in him
shall not perish but have eternal life. For
God did not send his Son into the world to
condemn the world, but to save the world
through him.

—JOHN 3:16, 17

*For it is by grace
you have been
saved, through
faith—
and this not from
yourselves, it is the
gift of God—not
by works, so that
no one can boast.*

—EPHESIANS 2:8, 9

Hope

"For I know the plans I have for you," declares the
LORD, "plans to prosper you and not to harm
you, plans to give you hope and a future."

—JEREMIAH 29:11

Find rest, O my soul, in God alone; my hope comes from him.
He alone is my rock and my salvation; he is my fortress, I will not be shaken.
My salvation and my honor depend on God; he is my mighty rock, my refuge.
Trust in him at all times, O people; pour out your hearts to him, for God is our refuge.

—PSALM 62:5-8

I lift up my eyes to the hills—where does my help come from?
My help comes from the LORD, the Maker of heaven and earth.
He will not let your foot slip—he who watches over you will not slumber.

—PSALM 121:1-3

Why are you downcast, O my soul? Why so disturbed within me?
Put your hope in God, for I will yet praise him, my Savior and my God.

—PSALM 42:11

Confusion

Dear friends, do not believe every spirit, but test the spirits to see whether they are from God, because many false prophets have gone out into the world. This is how you can recognize the Spirit of God: Every spirit that acknowledges that Jesus Christ has come in the flesh is from God. —1 JOHN 4:1, 2

So do not fear, for I am with you; do not be dismayed, for I am your God. I will strengthen you and help you; I will uphold you with my righteous right hand.   —ISAIAH 41:10

The fear of the LORD is the beginning of wisdom; all who follow his precepts have good understanding. To him belongs eternal praise.   —PSALM 111:10

Do not conform any longer to the pattern of this world, but be transformed by the renewing of your mind. Then you will be able to test and approve what God's will is—his good, pleasing and perfect will.   —ROMANS 12:2

Guidance

But when he, the Spirit of truth, comes, he will guide you into all truth. He will not speak on his own; he will speak only what he hears, and he will tell you what is yet to come.
                                —JOHN 16:13

I will lead the blind by ways they have not known, along unfamiliar paths I will guide them; I will turn the darkness into light before them and make the rough places smooth. These are the things I will do; I will not forsake them.
                                —ISAIAH 42:16

If I rise on the wings of the dawn, if I settle on the far side of the sea, even there your hand will guide me, your right hand will hold me fast. If I say, "Surely the darkness will hide me and the light become night around me," even the darkness will not be dark to you; the night will shine like the day, for darkness is as light to you.
                                —PSALM 139:9-12

In his heart a man plans his course, but the LORD determines his steps.   —PROVERBS 16:9

God's Goodness and Mercy

But I pray to you, O LORD, in the time of your favor; in your great love, O God, answer me with your sure salvation. Rescue me from the mire, do not let me sink; deliver me from those who hate me, from the deep waters. Do not let the floodwaters engulf me or the depths swallow me up or the pit close its mouth over me. Answer me, O LORD, out of the goodness of your love; in your great mercy turn to me. Do not hide your face from your servant; answer me quickly, for I am in trouble.

—PSALM 69:13-17

Who is a God like you, who pardons sin and forgives the transgression of the remnant of his inheritance? You do not stay angry forever but delight to show mercy.

—MICAH 7:18

Grace and peace be yours in abundance through the knowledge of God and of Jesus our Lord. His divine power has given us everything we need for life and godliness through our knowledge of him who called us by his own glory and goodness. Through these he has given us his very great and precious promises, so that through them you may participate in the divine nature and escape the corruption in the world caused by evil desires.

—2 PETER 1:2-4

And we know that in all things God works for the good of those who love him, who have been called according to his purpose.

—ROMANS 8:28

God's Provision

The LORD is my shepherd, I shall not be in want.

—PSALM 23:1

Then Jesus declared, "I am the bread of life. He who comes to me will never go hungry, and he who believes in me will never be thirsty."

—JOHN 6:35

He who did not spare his own Son, but gave him up for us all—how will he not also, along with him, graciously give us all things?

—ROMANS 8:32

> *Therefore I tell you, whatever you ask for in prayer, believe that you have received it, and it will be yours.*
>
> —MARK 11:24

God's Forgiveness

If we confess our sins, he is faithful and just and will forgive us our sins and purify us
from all unrighteousness.

—1 JOHN 1:9

When you were dead in your sins and in the uncircumcision of your sinful nature, God
made you alive with Christ. He forgave us all our sins, having canceled the written
code, with its regulations, that was against us and that stood opposed to us; he took it
away, nailing it to the cross.

—COLOSSIANS 2:13, 14

Praise the LORD, O my soul, and forget not all his benefits—who forgives all your sins
and heals all your diseases, who redeems your life from the pit and crowns you with
love and compassion.

—PSALM 103:2-4

The LORD is compassionate and gracious, slow to anger, abounding in love. He will not
always accuse, nor will he harbor his anger forever; He does not treat us as our sins
deserve or repay us according to our iniquities. For as high as the heavens are above
the earth, so great is his love for those who fear him;
As far as the east is from the west, so far has he removed our transgressions from us.

—PSALM 103:8-12

Temptation

So, if you think you are standing firm, be careful that you don't fall! No temptation has
seized you except what is common to man. And God is faithful; he will not let you be
tempted beyond what you can bear. But when you are tempted, he will also provide a
way out so that you can stand up under it.

—1 CORINTHIANS 10:12, 13

Because he himself suffered when he was tempted, he is able to help those who are
being tempted.

—HEBREWS 2:18

Finally, be strong in the Lord and in his mighty power. Put on the full armor of
God so that you can take your stand against the devil's schemes. For our struggle
is not against flesh and blood, but against the rulers, against the authorities, against
the powers of this dark world and against the spiritual forces of evil in the
heavenly realms.

—EPHESIANS 6:10-12

Blessed is the man who perseveres under trial, because when he has stood the test, he
will receive the crown of life that God has promised to those who love him.

—JAMES 1:12

God's Presence

When you pass through the waters, I will be with you; and when you pass through the rivers, they will not sweep over you. When you walk through the fire, you will not be burned; the flames will not set you ablaze.

—ISAIAH 43:2

The LORD is near to all who call on him, to all who call on him in truth. He fulfills the desires of those who fear him; he hears their cry and saves them.

—PSALM 145:18, 19

We are hard pressed on every side, but not crushed; perplexed, but not in despair; persecuted, but not abandoned; struck down, but not destroyed.

—2 CORINTHIANS 4:8, 9

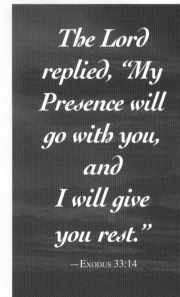

The Lord replied, "My Presence will go with you, and I will give you rest."

—EXODUS 33:14

Anger

"In your anger do not sin": Do not let the sun go down while you are still angry, and do not give the devil a foothold.

—EPHESIANS 4:26, 27

My dear brothers, take note of this: Everyone should be quick to listen, slow to speak and slow to become angry, for man's anger does not bring about the righteous life that God desires.

—JAMES 1:19, 20

Do not repay anyone evil for evil. Be careful to do what is right in the eyes of everybody. If it is possible, as far as it depends on you, live at peace with everyone. Do not take revenge, my friends, but leave room for God's wrath, for it is written: "It is mine to avenge; I will repay," says the Lord.

—ROMANS 12:17-19

A man of knowledge uses words with restraint, and a man of understanding is even-tempered. Even a fool is thought wise if he keeps silent, and discerning if he holds his tongue.

—PROVERBS 17:27, 28

Understanding

If any of you lacks wisdom, he should ask God, who gives generously to all without finding fault, and it will be given to him.

—JAMES 1:5

Trust in the LORD with all your heart and lean not on your own understanding; In all your ways acknowledge him, and he will make your paths straight.

—PROVERBS 3:5, 6

"For my thoughts are not your thoughts, neither are your ways my ways," declares the LORD. "As the heavens are higher than the earth, so are my ways higher than your ways and my thoughts than your thoughts."

—ISAIAH 55:8, 9

"This is what the LORD says, he who made the earth, the LORD who formed it and established it—the LORD is his name: 'Call to me and I will answer you and tell you great and unsearchable things you do not know.'"

—JEREMIAH 33:2, 3

Sharing Your Faith

How beautiful on the mountains are the feet of those who bring good news, who proclaim peace, who bring good tidings, who proclaim salvation, who say to Zion, "Your God reigns!"

—ISAIAH 52:7

Then Jesus came to them and said, "All authority in heaven and on earth has been given to me. Therefore go and make disciples of all nations, baptizing them in the name of the Father and of the Son and of the Holy Spirit, and teaching them to obey everything I have commanded you. And surely I am with you always, to the very end of the age."

—MATTHEW 28:18-20

"You are the salt of the earth. But if the salt loses its saltiness, how can it be made salty again? It is no longer good for anything, except to be thrown out and trampled by men. You are the light of the world. A city on a hill cannot be hidden. Neither do people light a lamp and put it under a bowl. Instead they put it on its stand, and it gives light to everyone in the house. In the same way, let your light shine before men, that they may see your good deeds and praise your Father in heaven."

—MATTHEW 5:13-16

Jesus said, "I tell you, whoever acknowledges me before men, the Son of Man will also acknowledge him before the angels of God."

—LUKE 12:8

BIBLE PROMISES
FOR HOPE AND COURAGE

From the psalms and prophets of the Old Testament to the Gospels and letters of the New Testament, the Bible contains promises from God that can comfort us in times of pain, give us strength in times of weakness, and give us hope in times of despair.

God's love is revealed in every page of Scripture. Every promise made is a window into the heart of the Ever-Present, Sovereign, Almighty God.

Jesus said, "Come to me, all you who are weary and burdened, and I will give you rest."

—MATTHEW 11:28

I lift up my eyes to the hills—where does my help come from?
My help comes from the Lord, the Maker of heaven and earth.
He will not let your foot slip—he who watches over you will not slumber.

—PSALM 121:1-3

But those who hope in the Lord will renew their strength. They will soar on wings like eagles; they will run and not grow weary, they will walk and not be faint.

—ISAIAH 40:31

Do not be anxious about anything, but in everything, by prayer and petition, with thanksgiving, present your requests to God. And the peace of God, which transcends all understanding, will guard your hearts and your minds in Christ Jesus.

—PHILIPPIANS 4:6, 7

Following
Jesus

Basics of Faith and Christian Living
Salvation, Sin, and Forgiveness
Prayer, Bible Study, and Church
Fears, Doubts, and Trust
Spiritual Gifts, Giving, and Sharing
Reliability of the Christian Faith

SALVATION, SIN & FORGIVENESS

Welcome to God's Family!

Now that you believe in Jesus Christ, you are a "child of God" and you belong to a new family. The goal of this family is to serve God and to love people. Some people think that Christianity is a set of rules. It is really a relationship between a loving God and his beloved children (Romans 5:6-11).

Here are some of the most common questions that Christians have . . .

How Can I Be Sure that I'm Saved?

A **The Bible tells us to:**
Admit we have sinned
(Romans 3:23; 6:23; 1 John 1:10)

B **Believe in Jesus** (John 1:12)

C **Confess that Jesus is Lord**
(Romans 10:9; Ephesians 2:8, 9)

Sometimes you may feel close to God, other times you may feel distant from him. Some people feel great joy and freedom from their problems when they first believe in Jesus. After a while, this joy may fade. This is normal.

Don't depend on your feelings. The Bible says, "*...if you confess with your mouth, "Jesus is Lord," and believe in your heart that God raised him from the dead, you will be saved*" (Romans 10:9).

Look for evidence of change. God now calls you his child, and has sent his Spirit to work inside you (John 1:12; 14:25, 26). As a follower of Jesus, you should see *progress*—not *perfection*—in your desire to obey and please Him (Ecclesiastes 7:20; Romans 7:14-25). For example, before you became a Christian you lost your temper or lied or hated people and it did not bother you. Now you have a deep desire to change and you regret your failures.

Hang in there! When you're discouraged by doubts and failures, remember that growth is a process. God has plans for you, and won't give up on you—ask for God's help. God promises to help you improve (Philippians 1:6).

Can God Forgive Me?

Yes! God can forgive any sin, no matter how terrible—cheating, murder, lying, infidelity, gossip, theft, selfishness. All people fail and disobey God. No one measures up. In fact the Bible says that no one can please God by good deeds. Good deeds aren't good enough.

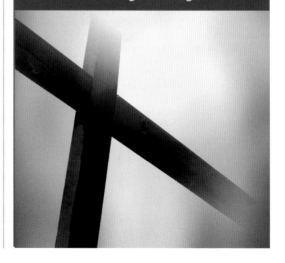

God promises that he will forgive you.
If we confess our sins, he is faithful and just and will forgive us our sins and purify us from all unrighteousness (1 John 1:9).

Jesus once told a story to his disciples, warning them that "good people" who think they are good enough for God are in more spiritual danger than humble people who recognize that they are unworthy and ask for forgiveness (Luke 18:9-14).

Confess your sins and forgive others.
Though God has forgiven you, you'll still have struggles. Some consequences and scars from your past may remain. If you've wronged others, ask for their forgiveness and try to make amends (with counsel from mature believers). When others wrong you, God asks that you forgive them—not because they deserve it, but out of gratitude for the great gift you received from God (Colossians 3:13).

What If I Sin?

Don't be surprised by your struggles. Everyone has them. The Bible says
... for all have sinned and fall short of the glory of God, and are justified freely by his grace through the redemption that came by Christ Jesus (Romans 3:23, 24).

Every follower of Jesus has certain vulnerabilities, whether it is losing your temper, materialism, envy, gossip, or pornography. People may persuade you to disobey God, or you may find yourself in tempting situations. The Bible says that before you accept Jesus, it is very difficult for you to resist temptation (Colossians 1:13). Even after deciding to follow Jesus, people still struggle with temptation and sometimes give into temptation. The good news is, once you've decided to follow Jesus, you will possess the desire to please God daily, and God will continue to help you resist temptation (Romans 7:21-25).

All people sin. When you do sin, it's not the end of your relationship with God. Confess your wrongs to God, and he will forgive you. Find Christian friends and support one another.

No matter what happens, God promises you a way to escape any spiritual danger.
No temptation has seized you except what is common to man. And God is faithful; he will not let you be tempted beyond what you can bear. But when you are tempted, he will also provide a way out so that you can stand up under it (1 Corinthians 10:13).

PRAYER, BIBLE STUDY & CHURCH

How Do I Pray?

God wants to have a relationship with you! Prayer is simply "staying connected" with your heavenly Father by talking to him. It doesn't matter whether you're happy, puzzled, hurt, or in trouble; you can talk about anything with God. Trust that God wants the best for you. When you ask for things, God may say "yes," "no," or "not yet" (Romans 8:26-28).

God cares about you and will listen to you when you talk to him. *Do not be anxious about anything, but in everything, by prayer and petition, with thanksgiving, present your requests to God and the peace of God that passes all understanding will guard your hearts and minds in Christ Jesus* (Philippians 4:6, 7).

Where to pray. Jesus said you should find a secluded quiet place, and pray to God (Matthew 6:6). You can pray in your bedroom, car, or on a walk...anywhere. Try to set aside a special time each day to talk to God. Many people find that early morning is the best time to pray because there are fewer distractions. Start by praying for five to ten minutes and then increase the time you spend with God as your prayer life becomes more disciplined.

The Lord's Prayer. Jesus taught his disciples how to pray using the Lord's Prayer:

Our Father in heaven, hallowed be your name, your kingdom come, your will be done on earth as it is in heaven. Give us today our daily bread. Forgive us our debts, as we also have forgiven our debtors. And lead us not into temptation, but deliver us from the evil one.

The Lord's Prayer has four parts to help us remember:

- **PRAISE** Recognize that God is great and in charge. Remember, God loves you and knows what's best for you.
- **PROVIDE** Ask God to provide for you, your family, and friends. Ask for healing, courage, and wisdom for the problems you might have.
- **PARDON** Confess your sins and ask others for forgiveness. Remember to forgive people who have wronged you. Let God know that you are sorry for disobeying him and wronging other people. Ask for forgiveness; God promises to forgive you.
- **PROTECTION** We are constantly faced with temptation. Ask for God's protection and the strength to do what is right (Matthew 6:9-13).

How Do I Read the Bible?

Open It! In order to follow Jesus you need to know what he said and did.

Begin by reading the Gospels (stories of the life of Jesus):
- Matthew
- Luke
- Mark
- John

Apply It!

As you read, look for—
- An example to admire or avoid
- A command to obey
- A sin to confess
- A promise to embrace

With a mature believer, discuss the parts you don't understand. Read and pray (Acts 17:11).

Engage It! You may find it helpful to use a study Bible and take notes about what you read. It is important to read the Bible every day, because it has many passages that will give you encouragement. Memorizing these verses will be a big help to your life (Psalm 1:2; 119:15, 16).

It may be helpful to read:
- Genesis • Psalms
- Proverbs • Romans

Why is the Bible Important?
The Bible is the Word of God. It provides us with the wisdom needed in order to share with others the "good news" about Jesus. The Bible is useful for teaching others, recognizing incorrect teachings, and learning how to live as followers of Jesus day by day (2 Timothy 3:16, 17).

Do I Need to Go to Church?

A New Family. The church is made up of believers who become your family. The people at church care about you, support you, teach you, and encourage you.

The Lord wants believers to meet together.
And let us consider how we may spur one another on toward love and good deeds.

Let us not give up meeting together, as some are in the habit of doing, but let us encourage one another— and all the more as you see the Day approaching (Hebrews 10:24, 25).

A Special Niche. The Bible describes the church as a building where you fit like a custom-cut stone (1 Peter 2:4, 5). Every player on a sports team is necessary and important to the team as a whole. In the same way, you are important to the church, and other believers need you. Your unique strengths and gifts will help others. You may not like or agree with every other believer, but no Christian is perfect and neither are you.

Be forgiving and live at peace with other followers of Jesus.
Be completely humble and gentle; be patient, bearing with one another in love. Make every effort to keep the unity of the Spirit through the bond of peace (Ephesians 4:2, 3).

A Larger Purpose. When Jesus went to heaven, he told his followers to love each other. In fact, he said that other people would know you were a follower of Jesus if you loved other Christians.

This is not always easy. Some people have personalities that are hard to love. Perhaps they are judgmental or grumpy. Jesus calls us to treat them kindly and gently and care for them.

FEARS, DOUBTS & TRUST

What About Fears and Doubts?

The Fear Factor.
Do you ever worry about the future? How will I pay my bills? Will I ever get married? Will my children be safe? Will disaster strike? Life is better when we have someone strong and loving to lean on.

The Bible says that God will never abandon you.
"...the LORD your God goes with you; he will never leave you nor forsake you" (Deuteronomy 31:6).

20 Questions. Real Christians *can* have doubts. At times, they may question whether God actually exists or doubt some of the claims of the Christian faith.

The Bible is full of questioners! Jesus' disciple Thomas was not present when Jesus first appeared to the other disciples after he rose from the dead. Thomas said that he would not believe unless he could see and touch the holes in Jesus' hands and put his hand in Jesus' side. Thomas might have had doubts about Jesus, but he kept his mind and heart open to the truth. When Jesus did appear to Thomas, Thomas exclaimed, "My Lord and my God." It was his search for the Truth that led Thomas into a faith that he had never had before (John 20:19-28).

Having doubts and questions may spur you to seek out answers, which can only bring you closer to God. In addition, believing something without checking the Bible may put you in spiritual danger. Doubts and questions help protect believers from being misled or becoming stagnant and inactive in their walk with Jesus.

Can God Be Trusted?

Why do bad things happen? A broken heart, an illness, a death in the family, a lost job.... Problems do come to followers of Jesus. Some hurts result from our own selfishness while others may result from the behavior of others. Bad things happen simply because we do not live in a perfect world and because God wanted to give us free will—the freedom to choose right and wrong (Romans 8:18-23).

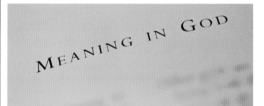

MEANING IN GOD

Is God really in control? Yes! God is with you, and he protects you more than you realize. When God does allow difficulties, it may be his way of disciplining you or strengthening you.

The Bible says that trials and sufferings help mold God's children into who God wants them to be. *Consider it pure joy, my brothers, whenever you face trials of many kinds, because you know that the testing of your faith develops perseverance. Perseverance must finish its work so that you may be mature and complete, not lacking anything* (James 1:2-4).

You may not recognize the purpose for problems in your life when they are occurring, but many times these trials could be part of a larger, unseen plan (John 9:1-3).

God has a good plan for you. *"For I know the plans I have for you," declares the LORD, "plans to prosper you and not to harm you, plans to give you hope and a future"* (Jeremiah 29:11).

Just before Jesus died on the cross, he earnestly asked God if it was possible to avoid it. However, Jesus ended his prayer by saying, "May *Your* will be done." Jesus also encouraged his followers to trust that God would take care of them (Matthew 6:25-34).

Why is the world such a mess?

If God condemns poverty and injustice, why does it go on? Evil has polluted everything and everyone God created (Jeremiah 17:9). Some skeptics say that either God is not loving or He is not powerful enough to stop evil. The truth is that God puts up with evil, but only for a while, because he is waiting with patience and love for people to return to him. A day of final judgment will come, when God will punish evil (2 Peter 3:1-10). God will make everything right and fair in the end.

What's My Purpose in Life?

The Big Picture. You were created to serve God and love the people around you. When asked what the greatest commandment was, Jesus replied: *"Love the Lord your God with all your heart and with all your soul and with all your mind." This is the first and greatest commandment. And the second is like it: "Love your neighbor as yourself"* (Matthew 22:37-39).

Ultimately, the purpose in life for believers is to worship God in everything we do. In addition, we are to care about other people and tell them about Jesus.

God cares about everyone, and longs for each person to be saved (1 Timothy 2:3, 4).

How Do You Fit In? You have a unique role in God's kingdom. The Bible says that God is the potter and you are the clay–the work of his hands (Isaiah 64:8). God knew you before you were born, and created you to have special qualities and talents for serving him. He shaped your background and circumstances, both good and bad (Psalm 139; Ephesians 2:10). Often, God uses the painful situations of the past to help others. For example, a widow may someday help a friend or lead a ministry that helps others go through grief.

Day by Day. How will you know what God wants you to do at each moment? Start by reading the Bible and obeying its teachings. Do your normal everyday responsibilities with a cheerful attitude and look for ways to serve others (Psalm 100:2). Pray for guidance and understanding. Your goal is to hear God say, "Good job" (Matthew 25:21).

SPIRITUAL GIFTS, GIVING & SHARING

What Are Spiritual Gifts and Talents?

You already had God-given talents before you decided to follow Jesus. Now you can use them for His glory—whether playing the guitar during worship, serving food in a homeless shelter, fixing the pastor's computer, leading a Bible study, or rocking babies in the church nursery.

Now, as a believer, you receive special gifts from God's Spirit to help His kingdom. *Each one should use whatever gift he has received to serve others, faithfully administering God's grace in its various forms* (1 Peter 4:10).

You may have a gift for preaching, teaching, or showing mercy. You may be good at encouraging others or noticing their needs. People may ask you for wise advice. The Bible lists many gifts (Romans 12; 1 Corinthians 12; Ephesians 4). To find your gifts, ask others what they think your gifts might be. Pray and try different ways of serving God. Though some gifts may seem better than others, the Bible is clear that every gift is important and necessary (Romans 12:3-8). No one should feel too important or unimportant; all gifts are needed for God's people to function as a team (1 Corinthians 12:4-31).

What about Giving?

Why should I give? Jesus gave his life for you (1 Corinthians 6:19, 20). Now you *and* all you own belong to him (Psalm 24:1). God wants our love and gratitude. We demonstrate our devotion to God by giving. Giving to God demonstrates that we are following Jesus and making him our "Number One" priority (Matthew 6:24).

Where should I give? You can advance God's cause in the world in many ways. You might give cash, a car, a computer, even a cow! Pastors, Christian workers, and missionaries need salaries. Church and outreach programs need money for buildings, books, utility bills, and more. And poor people, in your church or across the world, need help just to survive.

How do I give? Before you donate, ask if the money will be used wisely. Support the church you attend, and perhaps other causes as God stirs your heart. Contribute regularly and generously. A tenth of your income is the standard set up in the Old Testament.

When giving is tough, pray for God's help. God does promise to reward you in his own way whenever you give humbly and generously (Malachi 3:8-10, Matthew 6:1-4).

When you give with a cheerful attitude, God will give you all that you need.
Each man should give what he has decided in his heart to give, not reluctantly or under compulsion, for God loves a cheerful giver. And God is able to make all grace abound to you, so that in all things at all times, having all that you need, you will abound in every good work (2 Corinthians 9:7, 8).

How Do I Tell Others?

Start with your lifestyle. Actions speak louder than words! Jesus said that others will know Christians by their love for other people (John 13:35). Put other people's needs ahead of your own (Luke 10:27). With God's help, you can brighten your world with love and good deeds (Matthew 5:13-16).

Be prepared to talk about Jesus.
You never know when someone may ask (1 Peter 3:15).

God cares about people so much that he sent Jesus to save them and give them eternal life in heaven. Jesus said that, *"God so loved the world that he gave his one and only Son, that whoever believes in him shall not perish but have eternal life"* (John 3:16).

It would be helpful to mention a few Bible verses, such as:
- Romans 3:23: *...for all have sinned and fall short of the glory of God.*
- Romans 5:8, 9: *But God demonstrates his own love for us in this: While we were still sinners, Christ died for us.*
- Romans 6:23: *For the wages of sin is death, but the gift of God is eternal life in Christ Jesus our Lord.*

Share what God has done in your life. God promises to help you (1 Corinthians 2:11-13).

Look for opportunities. People can't learn about Jesus unless someone tells them (Romans 10:13-15). Pray for chances to share. Bring God into conversations naturally, talking about how you deal with problems or worries. Notice when others express spiritual hunger, and let them know what you have experienced. Treat them with gentleness and love, even if they are not open to the message (Colossians 4:6).

Leave matters in God's hands. You can't force someone to follow Jesus. You are responsible to share with and pray for others who don't know Jesus. God's Spirit can turn the most unlikely people to His Truth (Romans 10:1).

RELIABILITY OF THE CHRISTIAN FAITH

Is the Bible Reliable?

More than myths. More than 100 archaeological finds have confirmed the accuracy of the Bible. For example, scholars dismissed the biblical description of the Hittite nation as fiction until they found evidence (Joshua 1:1-4). The Bible's descriptions of cities, rulers, and battles match other historical records.

> **The Bible is inspired by God and is useful for teaching and equipping followers of Jesus to do God's work.**
> *All Scripture is God-breathed and is useful for teaching, rebuking, correcting and training in righteousness, so that the man of God may be thoroughly equipped for every good work* (2 Timothy 3:16, 17).

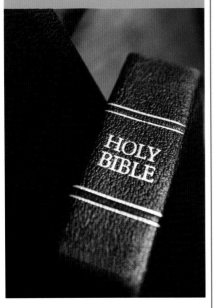

Accurately copied. Before the printing press, special scribes copied these texts by hand with an intricate checking system. The text of the Bible is better preserved than the writings of Plato and Aristotle. Discoveries like the Dead Sea Scrolls confirm their accuracy.

Is Following Jesus the Only Way to be Saved?

One way to God. Followers of Jesus claim to be a part of the one true religion and recognize the claims of Jesus as being true. Many people of other religions are good and moral people, but Jesus' own statements say that believing in him is the one and only way to be saved. In addition, the Bible is clear that being a moral person or doing good deeds is not enough to be saved.

> **Jesus said he was the only way to God.** Jesus said, *"I am the way and the truth and the life. No one comes to the Father except through me"* (John 14:6).

Jesus said that he provides people with eternal life. Jesus said, *"I give them eternal life, and they shall never perish; no one can snatch them out of my hand"* (John 10:28).

Jesus claimed to be God. Jesus said, *"I and the Father are one"* (John 10:30).

Being a good, sincere person is not enough. The Bible says, *"For it is by grace you have been saved, through faith—and this not from yourselves, it is the gift of God—not by works, so that no one can boast"* (Ephesians 2:8, 9).

Is There Evidence for the Resurrection?

Jesus was a real person. At least 39 ancient sources *apart from the Bible* note his teachings, miracles, life, and death.

Many saw him dead, then alive. Some say Jesus merely fainted on the cross. Others say the people who saw him alive later were "hallucinating." But Jesus' enemies and the Roman soldiers who executed him were satisfied that he was dead. Then after three days, 500 people, as individuals and in groups, morning and evening, indoors and outdoors, over a period of 40 days, saw and touched him as he walked, ate, and preached (1 Corinthians 15:3-8).

His followers changed radically. Jesus' disciples turned from "common people" into bold preachers, bravely facing persecution.

Most died as martyrs for their faith (Acts 4:1-22; 12:1-3). People would not die for a religious belief if they knew that belief was a lie.

Why does it matter? Jesus' resurrection proved he was divine and that everything he taught and claimed is true.

The resurrection of Jesus showed the penalty for sin was paid. It displayed God's power over death, and the new life he offers. *Praise be to the God and Father of our Lord Jesus Christ! In his great mercy he has given us new birth into a living hope through the resurrection of Jesus Christ from the dead* (1 Peter 1:3).

Jesus is our hope, who lives forever to present us as clean and pure before God (Hebrews 7:12-25).

The Journey

When you chose to follow Jesus, you embarked upon a journey that has high mountain peaks and occasional low valleys. The final destination is eternal life with God in heaven. The good news is that you are not left alone as you travel. You are following Jesus and He promises not to leave you behind. You also have several travelers alongside of you to encourage you and help carry your load.

Key Verses to Memorize

If you confess with your mouth, "Jesus is Lord," and believe in your heart that God raised him from the dead, you will be saved. —Romans 10:9

If we confess our sins, he is faithful and just and will forgive us our sins and purify us from all unrighteousness. —1 John 1:9

For all have sinned and fall short of the glory of God, and are justified freely by his grace through the redemption that came by Christ Jesus. —Romans 3:23, *24*

Do not be anxious about anything, but in everything, by prayer and petition, with thanksgiving, present your requests to God. And the peace of God, which transcends all understanding, will guard your hearts and your minds in Christ Jesus. —Philippians 4:6, 7

"For I know the plans I have for you," declares the LORD, "plans to prosper you and not to harm you, plans to give you hope and a future." —Jeremiah 29:11

Consider it pure joy, my brothers, whenever you face trials of many kinds, because you know that the testing of your faith develops perseverance. Perseverance must finish its work so that you may be mature and complete, not lacking anything. —James 1:2-4

The Great Commandment: *"Love the Lord your God with all your heart and with all your soul and with all your mind." This is the first and greatest commandment. And the second is like it: "Love your neighbor as yourself."* —Matthew 22:37-39

Each one should use whatever gift he has received to serve others, faithfully administering God's grace in its various forms. —1 Peter 4:10

God so loved the world that he gave his one and only Son, that whoever believes in him shall not perish but have eternal life. —John 3:16

For it is by grace you have been saved, through faith—and this not from yourselves, it is the gift of God—not by works, so that no one can boast. For we are God's workmanship, created in Christ Jesus to do good works, which God prepared in advance for us to do. —Ephesians 2:8-10

Contributor: Sue Gilliland

Bible
Translations
Comparison

Compare 20 Popular
Versions of the Bible

WHY ARE THERE SO MANY BIBLE TRANSLATIONS?

For more than 2000 years, scholars have been translating the Bible. The Old Testament was written over a 1500-year period before the birth of Christ. It was written primarily in Hebrew, with a few portions in Aramaic. The New Testament was written within 70 years of Christ's death and resurrection (AD 50-100). The writers of the New Testament wrote in *koine* Greek ("common" Greek).

The original manuscripts have not survived, but God's Word has been preserved through meticulous copying. Three primary methods of translation (and a fourth translation treatment) have evolved over the centuries:

• **Word-for-Word** – A process in which biblical and linguistic scholars attempt to translate each word based upon the word usage at the time of the writing. No translation is actually "word-for-word," but the intent is to come as close as possible.

• **Balance** – A process in which scholars attempt to mediate between a word-for-word approach and a thought-for-thought approach.

• **Thought-for-Thought** – A process in which scholars translate the meaning of each thought. This approach is also known as "dynamic equivalence." This is how most non-biblical translation for modern books is done.

• **Paraphrase** – A re-statement of a translation in modern terms and vocabulary, often expanded (or "amplified") for clarity.

Why Do New Translations Continue to Appear?

1. **Words change.** Modern language changes constantly, and the Bible must use understandable words for everyday life.

2. **Understanding of ancient languages changes.** The Bible was written using hundreds of words that are no longer understood. Scholars continue to discover the meanings of words and phrases, and either update or create new translations.

3. **Translators' purposes vary.** When an ancient word may be translated correctly in several different ways, the translators' purpose affects the words chosen.

BIBLE TRANSLATION
In order by date of release

TRANSLATION METHOD & READING LEVEL

YEAR
Year complete Bible was released

TRANSLATORS
Number of scholars and linguists involved in translating

SPONSOR
The organization(s) that helped sponsor the version

TEXTUAL BASIS
Which English Bible(s) and Greek and Hebrew manuscripts were used (see p.110)

PURPOSE
The purpose each translation was trying to accomplish

NOTABLE
Interesting facts

SAMPLE VERSE
Matthew 4:19 and John 3:16,17 as they are found in each version

KING JAMES VERSION (KJV)

AMERICAN STANDARD VERSION (ASV)

	KING JAMES VERSION (KJV)	AMERICAN STANDARD VERSION (ASV)
Method	**Word-for-word** Reading Grade Level: 12.0	**Word-for-word** Reading Grade Level: Unstated
Year	1611, current edition, 1769	1901
Translators	54 translators	30 American scholars who were part of the English Revised Version project in 1885
Sponsor	Six panels of translators appointed by King James I of England	British scholars from a variety of denominations
Textual Basis	Bishops Bible (1568) and Tyndale's Bible (1535) **Old Testament:** Masoretic Texts: Complutensian Polyglot and Antwerp Polygot **New Testament:** Textus Receptus	Derived from the English Revised Version (ERV) and the King James Version (KJV) **Old Testament:** Hebrew Masoretic Text, and Septuagint (see p. 110) **New Testament:** Westcott-Hort Greek New Testament
Purpose	In response to Protestant concerns of inaccuracies in earlier English versions (Tyndale, Geneva, Bishops)	To address approximately 300 suggestions from American translators to change the English Revised Version to acceptable American word use
Notable	The most widely printed and distributed version of the Bible. Used for devotional reading and Bible study by adults who prefer the English found in older versions.	ASV has earned the reputation as being very true to the Greek and Hebrew texts. Very formal. Used for serious Bible study.
Sample Verse	And he saith unto them, Follow me, and I will make you fishers of men. —Matthew 4:19 For God so loved the world, that he gave his only begotten Son, that whosoever believeth in him should not perish, but have everlasting life. For God sent not his Son into the world to condemn the world; but that the world through him might be saved. —John 3:16, 17	And he saith unto them, Come ye after me, and I will make you fishers of men. —Matthew 4:19 For God so loved the world, that he gave his only begotten Son, that whosoever believeth on him should not perish, but have eternal life. For God sent not the Son into the world to judge the world; but that the world should be saved through him. —John 3:16, 17

REVISED STANDARD VERSION (RSV)

AMPLIFIED BIBLE (AMP)

	RSV	AMP
Method	**Word-for-word** Reading Grade Level: 10.0	**Word-for-word, plus amplification of meaning** Reading Grade Level: 11.0
Year	1952	1965
Sponsor Translators	32 translators	Frances E. Siewert and 12 others
	International Council of Religious Education	The Lockman Foundation/Zondervan
Textual Basis	Based on the American Standard Version (ASV) **Old Testament:** Masoretic Text, Dead Sea Scrolls, Septuagint **New Testament:** Nestle-Aland text	Derived from the American Standard Version (ASV) **Old Testament:** Rudolf Kittel's Biblia Hebraica, Dead Sea Scrolls, Septuagint **New Testament:** Westcott-Hort Greek New Testament Nestle-Aland Novum Testamentum Graece (26th Edition)
Purpose	To preserve the best of the English Bible versions that preceded it	To allow the reader to better understand the meaning of words as they were used in their original context
Notable	Because the translation changed words such as "virgin" to "young woman," this version was criticized by conservatives.	Unique system of punctuation, typefaces, and synonyms (in parentheses) to more fully explain words. Used for devotional study.
Sample Verse	And he said to them, "Follow me, and I will make you fishers of men." —Matthew 4:19	And He said to them, Come after Me [as disciples--letting Me be your Guide], follow Me, and I will make you fishers of men! —Matthew 4:19
	For God so loved the world that he gave his only Son, that whoever believes in him should not perish but have eternal life. For God sent the Son into the world, not to condemn the world, but that the world might be saved through him. —John 3:16, 17	For God so greatly loved and dearly prized the world that He [even] gave up His only begotten (unique) Son, so that whoever believes in (trusts in, clings to, relies on) Him shall not perish (come to destruction, be lost) but have eternal (everlasting) life. For God did not send the Son into the world in order to judge (to reject, to condemn, to pass sentence on) the world, but that the world might find salvation and be made safe and sound through Him. —John 3:16, 17

NEW JERUSALEM BIBLE (NJB)

NEW AMERICAN BIBLE (NAB)

	NEW JERUSALEM BIBLE (NJB)		NEW AMERICAN BIBLE (NAB)
Method	Word-for-word Reading Grade Level: 9.0		Word-for-word Reading Grade Level: 6.6 
Year	1966, updated in 1985		1970, updated in 2000
Translators	36 translators		55 translators
Sponsor	Roman Catholic Church		Catholic Biblical Association of America
Textual Basis	Based upon a 1961 French translation La Bible de Jérusalem **Old Testament:** Masoretic Text, Septuagint **New Testament:** Eclectic Greek Texts		**Old Testament:** Masoretic Text, Septuagint, Vulgate, Dead Sea Scrolls, Hebrew text behind the Liber Psalmorum **New Testament:** Nestle-Aland Novum Testamentum Graece (26th Edition) and United Bible Societies' Greek New Testament (3rd Edition)
Purpose	A response to Pope Pius XII's request for a more clear, skilled translation by Dominicans and others at École Biblique in Jerusalem		A response to Pope Pius XII's request for a more clear, skilled translation by the Catholic Biblical Association of America
Notable	J.R.R. Tolkien, author of *The Lord of the Rings,* was one of the contributing translators. Includes the Apocrypha. Typically used by adult Roman Catholics for serious Bible study.		The official translation used in U.S. Catholic Church Mass. Includes the Apocrypha. Widely used by Roman Catholics of all ages for daily devotional reading and Bible study.
Sample Verse	And he said to them, "Come after me, and I will make you fishers of people." —Matthew 4:19 For this is how God loved the world: he gave his only Son, so that everyone who believes in him may not perish but may have eternal life. For God sent his Son into the world not to judge the world, but so that through him the world might be saved. —John 3:16, 17		He said to them, "Come after me, and I will make you fishers of men." —Matthew 4:19 For God so loved the world that he gave his only Son, so that everyone who believes in him might not perish but might have eternal life. For God did not send his Son into the world to condemn the world, but that the world might be saved through him. —John 3:16, 17

NEW AMERICAN STANDARD BIBLE (NASB)

GOOD NEWS TRANSLATION (GNT)

	NEW AMERICAN STANDARD BIBLE (NASB)		GOOD NEWS TRANSLATION (GNT)
Method	**Word-for-word** Reading Grade Level: 11.0		**Thought-for-thought** Reading Grade Level: 6.0
Year	1971, revised in 1995		1976
Translators	54 translators		R. Bratcher (New Testament) plus six others (Old Testament)
Sponsor	The Lockman Foundation		American Bible Society
Textual Basis	**Old Testament:** Rudolf Kittel's Biblia Hebraica (3rd Edition) Dead Sea Scrolls **New Testament:** Nestle-Aland Novum Testamentum Graece (26th Edition)		**Old Testament:** Biblia Hebraica **New Testament:** United Bible Societies' Greek New Testament
Purpose	To remove antiquated phrases and words, and to add modern punctuation		To provide a Bible for non-native English speakers
Notable	If the literal definition for an expression was determined to be unclear for contemporary readers, an equivalent modern expression was used. The more literal expression is described more fully in the footnotes. Used by adults for serious Bible study.		Endorsed by many evangelistic and denominational groups. Used by children and believers for whom English is not their first language.
Sample Verse	And He said to them, "Follow Me, and I will make you fishers of men." —Matthew 4:19 For God so loved the world, that He gave His only begotten Son, that whoever believes in Him shall not perish, but have eternal life. For God did not send the Son into the world to judge the world, but that the world might be saved through Him. —John 3:16, 17		Jesus said to them, "Come with me, and I will teach you to catch people." —Matthew 4:19 For God loved the world so much that he gave his only Son, so that everyone who believes in him may not die but have eternal life. For God did not send his Son into the world to be its judge, but to be its savior. —John 3:16, 17

NEW INTERNATIONAL VERSION (NIV)

NEW KING JAMES VERSION (NKJV)

	NIV		NKJV
Method	**Balance** between word-for-word and thought-for-thought Reading Grade Level: 7.0		**Word-for-word** Reading Grade Level: 9.0
Year	1978		1982
Translators	115 translators		119 translators
Sponsor	New York Bible Society (now known as International Bible Society)		Conceived by Arthur Farstad, commissioned by Thomas Nelson Publishers
Textual Basis	**Old Testament:** Biblia Hebraica, Dead Sea Scrolls, Septuagint, Aquila, Symmachus and Theodotian, Vulgate, and other ancient manuscripts **New Testament:** Eclectic text (see p. 110)		Derived from the King James Version (KJV) **Old Testament:** Masoretic Text **New Testament:** Textus Receptus Footnotes: Nestle-Aland text
Purpose	To provide a modern translation that would be acceptable to many denominations		To produce a modern language translation that would maintain the structure and beauty of the KJV
Notable	Currently the best-selling Bible version. Used by teenagers and adults for personal devotions, worship, and Bible study.		Indicates where other Greek and Hebrew manuscripts differ. Used for devotional reading and Bible study by adults who prefer the English found in older versions.
Sample Verse	"Come, follow me," Jesus said, "and I will make you fishers of men." —Matthew 4:19		Then He said to them, "Follow Me, and I will make you fishers of men." —Matthew 4:19
	For God so loved the world that he gave his one and only Son, that whoever believes in him shall not perish but have eternal life. For God did not send his Son into the world to condemn the world, but to save the world through him. —John 3:16, 17		For God so loved the world that He gave His only begotten Son, that whoever believes in Him should not perish but have everlasting life. For God did not send His Son into the world to condemn the world, but that the world through Him might be saved. —John 3:16, 17

(see p. 110)

NEW CENTURY VERSION (NCV)

NEW REVISED STANDARD VERSION (NRSV)

	NCV		NRSV
Method	Thought-for-thought Reading Grade Level: 5.6		Word-for-word Reading Grade Level: 8.0
Year	1987		1989
Translators	50+ translators		30 translators
Sponsor	World Bible Translation Center		Division of Christian Education and National Council of Churches
Textual Basis	**Old Testament:** Biblia Hebraica and the Septuagint **New Testament:** United Bible Societies' Greek New Testament (3rd Edition)		Derived from the Revised Standard Version and used the latest discovered texts **Old Testament:** Biblia Hebraica Stuttgartensia (1st Edition), Dead Sea Scrolls, Septuagint, Vulgate, Syriac Peshitta, Aramaic Targums **New Testament:** United Bible Societies' Greek New Testament (3rd Edition)
Purpose	To make a readable version that uses modern terms such as measurements and geographic names		To revise the Revised Standard Version using information gathered from newly discovered Hebrew and Greek manuscripts
Notable	Use of footnotes to clarify ancient customs and other concepts requiring special explanation. Widely used by children and teenagers for personal devotional reading.		Despite concerns by some Protestant groups about inclusive language, the NRSV was officially accepted by Episcopal, Presbyterian and U.S. and Canadian Catholic Bishops. "Gender neutral" in references on the human level (changing "mankind" to "humankind"), while maintaining masculine references to God.

Sample Verse

Jesus said, "Come follow me, and I will make you fish for people."
—Matthew 4:19

God loved the world so much that he gave his one and only Son so that whoever believes in him may not be lost, but have eternal life. God did not send his Son into the world to judge the world guilty, but to save the world through him.
—John 3:16, 17

And he said to them, "Follow me, and I will make you fish for people." —Matthew 4:19

For God so loved the world that he gave his only Son, so that everyone who believes in him may not perish but may have eternal life. Indeed, God did not send the Son into the world to condemn the world, but in order that the world might be saved through him.
—John 3:16, 17

CONTEMPORARY ENGLISH VERSION (CEV)

GOD'S WORD (GW)

	CEV	GW
Method	**Thought-for-thought** Reading Grade Level: 5.4	**Balance** between word-for-word and thought-for-thought Reading Grade Level: 4.5
Year	1995	1995
Translators	100+ translators (including reviewers)	New Testament: William F. Beck; Old Testament: Small group of Lutheran scholars
Sponsor	American Bible Society	God's Word to the Nations Bible Society
Textual Basis	**Old Testament:** Biblia Hebraica Stuttgartensia (4th Edition), the Septuagint **New Testament:** United Bible Societies' Greek New Testament (3rd Edition)	Revision of Beck's The New Testament in the Language of Today (1963) **Old Testament:** Biblia Hebraica Stuttgartensia **New Testament:** Nestle-Aland Novum Testamentum Graece
Purpose	To translate the Bible into the speech patterns found in modern communication	To remain loyal to the original manuscripts, yet use natural English
Notable	Recommended for children and people who do not speak English as a first language.	The translation was performed by full-time Bible scholars working with English editorial reviewers who helped balance the integrity of the translation with readability and relevance for today's English-speaking audience. Appropriate for children and new believers.
Sample Verse	Jesus said to them, "Come with me! I will teach you how to bring in people instead of fish." —Matthew 4:19	Jesus said to them, "Come, follow me! I will teach you how to catch people instead of fish." —Matthew 4:19
	God loved the people of this world so much that he gave his only Son, so that everyone who has faith in him will have eternal life and never really die. God did not send his Son into the world to condemn its people. He sent him to save them! —John 3:16, 17	God loved the world this way: He gave his only Son so that everyone who believes in him will not die but will have eternal life. God sent his Son into the world, not to condemn the world, but to save the world. —John 3:16, 17

NEW INTERNATIONAL READER'S VERSION (NIrV)

NEW LIVING TRANSLATION (NLT)

	NEW INTERNATIONAL READER'S VERSION (NIrV)		NEW LIVING TRANSLATION (NLT)
Method	**Thought-for-thought** Reading Grade Level: 2.9		**Thought-for-thought** Reading Grade Level: 6.3
Year	1996, revised in 1998		1996, revised in 2004
Translators	40 scholars (including some of the original NIV translators)		90 translators
Sponsor	International Bible Society and Zondervan Publishing House		Tyndale House Publishers
Textual Basis	New International Version		The Living Bible (1971) **Old Testament:** Biblia Hebraica Stuttgartensia (1977 Edition), Dead Sea Scrolls, the Septuagint, Vulgate, Syriac Peshitta, Samaritan Pentateuch **New Testament:** United Bible Societies' Greek New Testament (1977 Edition) Nestle-Aland (27th Edition)
Purpose	To provide a translation with simple words and short sentences to appeal to a lower reading level		To provide an easy-to-read modern version
Notable	The 1996 version contained gender inclusive language, but it was removed from the 1998 edition. This translation has the lowest reading level of any English translation on the market. Used by children for devotionals and worship.		A translation in the style of the Living Bible (TLB). Removes theological terms such as "justification," using the definition instead for clarity. Used by teenagers and adults for personal devotions, worship, and Bible study.
Sample Verse	"Come. Follow me," Jesus said. "I will make you fishers of people." —Matthew 4:19		Jesus called out to them, "Come, be my disciples, and I will show you how to fish for people!" —Matthew 4:19
	God loved the world so much that he gave his one and only Son. Anyone who believes in him will not die but will have eternal life. God did not send his Son into the world to judge the world. He sent his Son to save the world through him. —John 3:16, 17		For God loved the world so much that he gave his one and only Son, so that everyone who believes in him will not perish but have eternal life. God sent his Son into the world not to judge the world, but to save the world through him. —John 3:16, 17

ENGLISH STANDARD VERSION (ESV)		THE MESSAGE (MSG)
Word-for-word Reading Grade Level: 8.0 	Method	**Paraphrase** Reading Grade Level: 6.0 
2001	Year	2002
100+ translators	Translators	Eugene Peterson
Good News/Crossway Board of Directors	Sponsor	NavPress
Derived from Revised Standard Version **Old Testament:** Biblia Hebraica Stuttgartensia (2nd Ed.), Dead Sea Scrolls, Septuagint, Samaritan Pentateuch, Syriac Peshitta, Vulgate **New Testament:** United Bible Societies' Greek New Testament (4th Edition) and Nestle-Aland Novum Testamentum Graece (27th Edition)	Textual Basis	**Old Testament:** Biblia Hebraica **New Testament:** Greek New Testament
To produce a modern, readable and accurate translation in the tradition of the Tyndale Version (1535) and King James Version (1611)	Purpose	To re-create the common language in which the Bible was written into today's common language
Theologically conservative. Inclusive language (see p. 110) was typically avoided. Used by teenagers and adults for serious Bible study.	Notable	Intended to be used as an aid to understanding traditional Bible translations. Used for devotional reading.
And he said to them, "Follow me, and I will make you fishers of men." —Matthew 4:19 For God so loved the world, that he gave his only Son, that whoever believes in him should not perish but have eternal life. For God did not send his Son into the world to condemn the world, but in order that the world might be saved through him. —John 3:16, 17	Sample Verse	This is how much God loved the world: He gave his Son, his one and only Son. And this is why: so that no one need be destroyed; by believing in him, anyone can have a whole and lasting life. God didn't go to all the trouble of sending his Son merely to point an accusing finger, telling the world how bad it was. He came to help, to put the world right again. Anyone who trusts in him is acquitted; anyone who refuses to trust him has long since been under the death sentence without knowing it. And why? Because of that person's failure to believe in the one-of-a-kind Son of God when introduced to him. —John 3:16, 17

HOLMAN CHRISTIAN STANDARD BIBLE (HCSB)

TODAY'S NEW INTERNATIONAL VERSION (TNIV)

Method

Balance between word-for-word and thought-for-thought
Reading Grade Level: 7.5

Balance between word-for-word and thought-for-thought
Reading Grade Level: Unstated

Year

2004

2005

Translators

100 translators

115 translators

Sponsor

Conceived by Arthur Farstad and LifeWay Christian Resources of the Southern Baptist Convention; overseen by Holman Bible Publishers

Committee on Bible Translation

Textual Basis

Old Testament: Biblia Hebraica Stuttgartensia (5th Edition)
New Testament: Nestle-Aland Novum Testamentum Graece (27th Edition), United Bible Societies' Greek New Testament (4th Edition)

New International Version (NIV)
Old Testament: Biblia Hebraica, Dead Sea Scrolls, Septuagint, Aquila, Symmachus and Theodotian, Vulgate, and other ancient manuscripts
New Testament: Nestle-Aland (27th Edition) and United Bible Societies' Greek New Testaments (4th Edition)

Purpose

To make the most readable text possible while maintaining the integrity of the translation

To enhance the overall clarity of the NIV

Notable

Consistent and unique use of six English renderings for names of God: God (Elohim), LORD (YHWH), Lord (Adonai), Lord God (Adonai YHWH), Lord of Hosts (YHWH Sabaoth), God Almighty (El Shaddai). Alternative translations included in footnotes. Used by teenagers and adults for personal devotions and Bible Study.

Uses gender neutral terms wherever the original language suggests that the writer was referring to members of both genders: "And when they were created, he called them 'man'" (Genesis 5:2, NIV) is translated as "And when they were created, he called them 'human beings'" (TNIV). Used by teenagers and new believers for personal devotional reading and Bible study.

Sample Verse

"Follow Me," He told them, "and I will make you fish for people!" —Matthew 4:19

For God loved the world in this way: He gave His One and Only Son, so that everyone who believes in Him will not perish but have eternal life. For God did not send His Son into the world that He might judge the world, but that the world might be saved through Him.
—John 3:16, 17

"Come, follow me," Jesus said, "and I will send you out to fish for people." —Matthew 4:19

For God so loved the world that he gave his one and only Son, that whoever believes in him shall not perish but have eternal life. For God did not send his Son into the world to condemn the world, but to save the world through him.
—John 3:16, 17

THE THREE MOST POPULAR GREEK TEXTS

When translating the Bible from Greek, scholars examine one or more Greek texts of the New Testament. Each text varies slightly. It is important that scholars show the text or texts they are using and how they deal with the differences. Below are the three most popular texts used.

	Received Text ("Textus Receptus")	Westcott-Hort	Nestle-Aland United Bible Societies
Grouping	Based on Majority Text, Traditional Text, and Byzantine Text	Based on Alexandrian Text	Also known as Novum Testamentum Graece, Greek New Testament, and "Critical Text"
Date	1516: Several Greek New Testaments published by various scholars (Erasmus, Stephanus, Beza, Elzevirs)	1881: Westcott-Hort was the standard Greek text until 1945.	Latest editions; • 1993: Nestle-Aland, 27th Ed. • 1983: UBS, 4th Rev. Ed.
Foundation for	• KJV • NKJV	• ERV • ASV	• ESV • NASB • AMP • RSV • NRSV • JB • NCV • NLT • GNT • NIV • TNIV • CEV • TM • NAB • HCSB • NIrV
Based on which manuscripts?	• A few Byzantine text-type manuscripts dating from AD 1100 - AD 1300 (see p. 110). • Some of the book of Revelation was translated back into Greek from the Latin Vulgate because there were no Greek manuscripts of Revelation available to the translators at that time.	Alexandrian text-type manuscripts: • Codex Vaticanus (dated around AD 325, it had been in the Vatican library since at least 1478, but not released until the mid-19th century.) • Codex Sinaiticus (dated around AD 350, found in 1859) • Codex Alexandrinus (dated around AD 425 was discovered and locked away in Alexandria for several centuries and then made available to western scholars in 1629.)	• An eclectic text based on Byzantine text-type and Alexandrian text-type manuscripts depending upon which ones are the most reliable. Text reliability was assessed by examining external evidence (date, source, amount, relationship to other manuscripts) and internal evidence (the text itself). • Several newly discovered manuscripts such as the Oxyrhynchus Papyri (1898), the Chester Beatty Papyri (1930), and the Bodmer Papyri (1955).
Supporters say	• Based on the Majority Text, the only manuscripts available prior to AD 1516. • Appears to agree with early copies of the New Testament dating before AD 200. • A large number of Byzantine text-type manuscripts exists, however, only a few are ancient (before AD 600). Some suggest that humid climates caused the manuscripts to deteriorate.	• Based on the earliest manuscripts available by AD 1881. • Alexandrian text-type manuscripts were a result of scribes using reliable texts and careful copying. • Alexandrian text-type manuscripts are older, but only a few have been discovered. Some suggest that this is related to the decline of the Greek language and culture in Egypt after the 4th century.	• Scholars believe they have used the most reliable portions from all of the manuscripts (Byzantine, Alexandrian, and "Western"), including the most recently discovered papyri (e.g., Bodmer Papyri in 1955).
Critics say	• Erasmus did not have the Greek manuscripts discovered after 1518. • Consulted no more than six Greek manuscripts. • Includes variants found in only one 13th-century manuscript. (Erasmus doubted this manuscript's authenticity in his Annotations.) • Erasmus had to use portions of the Vulgate to create the Textus Receptus, making it a translation of a translation. • Byzantine text-type derives from the Lucianic text, which went through substantive editing in order to create a harmonious and smooth text. • Some scholars argue that Byzantine text-type manuscripts have been influenced by Arian teachings.	• The translators did not consider the majority texts (Byzantine text-type manuscripts). • Was not able to use manuscripts discovered after 1881 such as Oxyrhynchus, Chester Beatty, and Bodmer Papyri. These papyri are dated earlier than previous manuscripts and some scholars consider them to be the most reliable manuscripts available today. • A few scholars argue that Alexandrian text-type manuscripts have been influenced by Egyptian pagan and Gnostic teachings.	• A few scholars argue that Alexandrian text-type manuscripts have been influenced by Egyptian pagan and Gnostic teachings. **What is a Study Bible?** Bibles such as the Life Application Bible or the Open Bible are a combination of (1) a Bible translation and (2) notes by scholars. These notes usually explain the culture, history, language, and text variants, and compare biblical passages.

IMPORTANT WORDS TO KNOW

- **Apocrypha** – Several books and additions that were included in the early Greek and Latin translations of the Old Testament. However, recent evidence revealed that the Hebrew canon did not include the Apocrypha. This evidence lead to its removal from the Geneva Bible in AD 1640. By AD 1827, the Apocrypha is omitted from most Protestant versions of the Bible.

- **Biblia Hebraica** – Latin for "Hebrew Bible." Contains many variances from the Masoretic Text based upon earlier translations and manuscript discoveries.

- **Dead Sea Scrolls** – Some of the oldest known copies of portions of Old Testament manuscripts, unearthed in the late 1940s near the Dead Sea, some dating as early as 125 BC.

- **Eclectic text** – Scholars examined every ancient Greek manuscript available, and then selected the variant that seemed best. Eclecticism practices textual criticism (examining external and internal evidence) in order to determine which variant is the most accurate to the original writing (autograph). In theory, eclecticism shows no favoritism for one text-type over the other. However, the oldest manuscripts (Alexandrian text-type) are typically favored.

- **Greek New Testament** – A general reference to one of many editions of the New Testament in the ancient Greek language of Jesus' day, known as *koine* Greek. These each have slight variations, and study Bibles usually list the differences. Most variations are in spellings and place names, none affect Christian doctrines.

- **Greek Text** – The New Testament was written in the kind of Greek that was spoken by common people at the time of Jesus and his disciples. The New Testament is the most well-documented written material from the first century. Several thousand manuscript copies of the New Testament books exist. Because these were copied by hand, there are slight differences (called "variants") between manuscripts. Scholars have put these manuscripts into groups, called text-types, based on the kinds of differences.

There are several major groups of Greek manuscripts:

1. **"Western" text-type (also called Popular text)** – These manuscripts were grouped together because they were hand copied before AD 400 and were not copied in Alexandria, Egypt.

2. **Lucianic text-type** – This manuscript group was edited by Lucian of Antioch c. AD 300. He started with the Western manuscripts and edited them to produce a smooth, harmonized copy of the New Testament. This was the most popular text-type after Constantine legalized Christianity, and it influenced the Byzantine manuscripts.

3. **Byzantine text-type** (also called Constantinopolitan, Syrian, Ecclesiastical, or Majority) – The largest number of surviving manuscripts fit into this group for any of three possible reasons: (A) These manuscripts were considered superior to Alexandrian manuscripts, (B) the manuscripts were more readily available and widely circulated when Christianity became legal under Emperor Constantine, or (C) Byzantine churches were the only churches in the Roman Empire that continued to copy manuscripts in Greek after the 4th century.

4. **Alexandrian text-type** (also Neutral or Egyptian) – The oldest manuscripts available today are in this group. They survived due to the dry climate of Egypt that preserved the writing material. The best known Alexandrian manuscripts are Codex Vaticanus, Codex Sinaiticus, Codex Alexandrinus, and the more recently discovered Oxyrhynchus, Chester Beatty, and Bodmer Papyri (dated before AD 300).

- **Inclusive language** – For Bible translation, it is language that neither refers to male or female (gender neutral), adult or child (age neutral) if the terms do not specify a gender or age. Translators who strive for inclusive language emphasize the gender neutrality of some Greek and Hebrew terms that have been traditionally translated with a masculine orientation.

- **Masoretic Text** – The name given to the texts carefully copied by generations of Jewish scholars using a strict set of proofreading guidelines.

- **Reading Grade Level** – The number corresponds with the educational grade level. For example, 7.5 means that the translation was geared for a person who has completed half of the seventh grade in school.

- **Septuagint** – A translation of the Old Testament into Greek, completed before the birth of Christ. Also called the LXX (the Latin numeral for 70, referring to the traditional belief that 70 translators worked on the Septuagint).

- **Textus Receptus** – Latin for "received text," this refers to the Greek New Testament assembled by Erasmus in the 1500s that provides the basis for Tyndale's New Testament, the King James Version, and the New King James Version.

- **Translation** – In Bible terms, the process of converting original language of the manuscripts (mainly Hebrew and Greek) into a modern language.

- **Vulgate** – A 5th-century translation of the Bible into Latin.

Contributors: Vincent Botticelli; Gary Burge, Ph.D.; G. Goldsmith; Timothy Paul Jones, Ed.D.; Shawn Vander Lugt, M.Div.

Thanks to: Scott Smith; Sam Fisher; Charles Cole; Pam McAskill; and Sarah Mahar.

Look for Other Rose Bible Basics Books

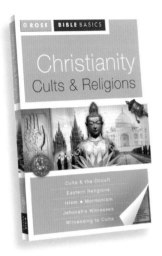

Christianity, Cults & Religions

Helps clarify differences between the beliefs and practices of various religions, cults, and new religious movements. Includes topics such as: Who is God? Who is Jesus Christ? What is salvation? What happens after death?

Contains comparisons of biblical Christianity with Anthroposophy, Bahá'í, Buddhism, Christian Science, Eastern mysticism, Hare Krishna, Hinduism, Islam, Jehovah's Witnesses, Judaism, Latter-day Saints/Mormons, Muslims, Nation of Islam, New age movement, Soka Gakkai International, Scientology (Dianetics), Theosophy, TM (Transcendental Meditation), Unification Church, Unity School, Wicca, Kabbalah, and more.

112 pages, 6 x 9-inch paperback.   ISBN: 9781596362024

Names of God and Other Bible Studies

Contains favorite Bible studies to use in small groups, church groups, and for individual study. Includes studies on the Names of God, Names of Jesus, Names of the Holy Spirit, Trinity, Ten Commandments, Lord's Prayer, Beatitudes, Fruit of the Spirit, and Armor of God. 112 pages. Includes color charts, illustrations, and photos throughout.

112 pages, 6 x 9-inch paperback.   ISBN: 9781596362031

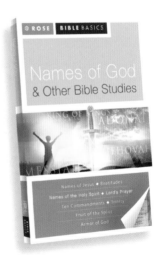

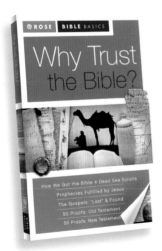

Why Trust the Bible?

Is the Bible an ancient document that has been tampered with? Has it been edited many times over the centuries and now is filled with errors? How can we know what the Bible really said when the originals no longer exist?

This book gives answers to the following claims by critics:
- The Gospels were written long after Jesus lived by people who weren't eyewitnesses.
- The stories about Jesus' life and death were not handed down reliably and not recorded accurately.
- The Bible is full of textual errors, as proven by the Dead Sea Scrolls.
- The New Testament wasn't finalized until hundreds of years after Jesus and his disciples, so there could have been many other "Gospels" accepted and later rejected in addition to the four Gospels found in the Bible today.
- The Bible was edited by people who had an "agenda" and changed many teachings.

112 pages, 6 x 9-inch paperback.   ISBN: 9781596362017

Other Rose Publishing Books

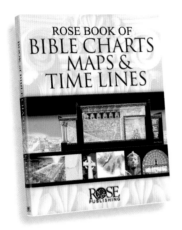

Rose Book of Bible Charts, Maps & Time Lines

Dozens of popular Rose Publishing Bible charts, maps, and time lines in one spiral-bound book. Reproduce up to 300 copies of any chart free of charge.

192 pages. Hardcover.   ISBN-13: 9781596360228

Deluxe "Then and Now" Bible Maps

Book with CD-ROM!
See where Bible places are today with "Then and Now" Bible maps with clear plastic overlays of modern cities and countries. This deluxe edition comes with a CD-ROM that gives you a JPG of each map to use in your own Bible material as well as PDFs of each map and overlay to create your own handouts or overhead transparencies. PowerPoint fans can create their own presentations with these digitized maps.

Hardcover. ISBN-13: 9781596361638

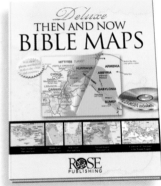

Rose Book of Bible & Christian History Time Lines

Six thousand years and 20 feet of time lines in one hard-bound cover! This unique resource allows you to easily store and reference two time lines in book form. These gorgeous time lines printed on heavy chart paper, can also be slipped out of their binding and posted in a hallway or large room for full effect.
• The 10-foot Bible Time Line compares Scriptural events with world history and Middle East history. Shows hundreds of facts; includes dates of kings, prophets, battles, and key events.
• The 10-foot Christian History Time Line begins with the life of Jesus and continues to the present day. Includes key people and events that all Christians should know. Emphasis on world missions, the expansion of Christianity, and Bible translation in other languages. These two time lines are connected end-to-end to form one long teaching aid.

Hardcover. ISBN-13: 9781596360846